LOUISIANA STATE UNIVERSITY STUDIES
Max Goodrich, General Editor

Social Science Series
Walter C. Richardson, Editor

Number Eleven
The United Nations Administrative Tribunal

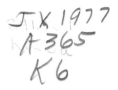

THE UNITED NATIONS ADMINISTRATIVE TRIBUNAL

Byung Chul Koh

LOUISIANA STATE UNIVERSITY PRESS / Baton Rouge, 1966

CONTENTS

LIST OF TABLES

ACKNOWLEDGMENTS

THE AUTHOR WOULD LIKE to acknowledge the help of some of those who made this study possible. His is a lasting debt of gratitude to Professor Paul P. Van Riper, chairman of his doctoral committee at Cornell University, not only for his doggedly persistent intellectual stimulation and guidance, but also for his equally untiring patience and understanding. Without his help and encouragement, this study could not have been completed. He is also deeply grateful to Professor Earl Brooks and Professor Herbert W. Briggs, members of his doctoral committee. By word and deed alike, Professor Brooks taught him how to approach, analyze, and assay the human problems of modern organizations. By the rigors of his scholarship, surpassed only by the warmth of his personality, Professor Briggs guided and inspired the writer's study of international law and organization.

Special thanks are due to Dr. Nicholas Teslenko, Executive Secretary of the United Nations Administrative Tribunal, and Mrs. Doriane Kurz, his secretary, for their invaluable assistance and cooperation while this study was under preparation. Not only did they willingly give many hours of their precious time to the endless inquiries by the writer; but they also helped him to gain access to many useful documents pertinent to the functioning of the Tribunal. It should also be noted, with gratitude, that Madame Paul Bastid, President of the Tribunal and Professor of Law at the University of Paris, has done the writer the singular honor of reading and commenting on the study in its entirety.

Finally, the writer is deeply grateful to the Graduate School of Business and Public Administration, the Cornell Graduate School, and the Cornell Social Science Research Center for their generous financial assistance.

THE UNITED NATIONS ADMINISTRATIVE TRIBUNAL

INTRODUCTION

THE IMPORTANCE OF the human factor in bureaucratic administration is a familiar theme in the literature of organizational theory. Not only does an organization depend on the expertise and devotion of its personnel for carrying out its day-to-day activities, but it can assert an institutional identity only through its professional staff. Bureaus, in themselves, do not make up a bureaucracy. Bureaucrats do.

These generalizations are no less germane to international administration. For, indeed, on the very shoulders of the men and women who staff the Secretariat of the United Nations rests the solemn task of keeping the Organization going and, better still, growing. They are, as Inis L. Claude, Jr., a noted student of international organization, points out, "the sole tangible evidence" of the continued existence of the United Nations, for "governmental representatives assemble and adjourn, leaving staff members in the headquarters building to provide proof that the 'United Nations' is something more than the expectation that the governments will meet again." [1]

Of the diverse and challenging problems connected with the personnel administration of the United Nations, one which has been little explored by scholars yet which is nonetheless significant and interesting, is that of legal protection of the international civil servant. Institutionally, this task is entrusted to the Administrative Tribunal of the United Nations. Clothed with authority to adjudicate disputes arising out of employment relations in the Organization, the Tribunal performs a dual task: it sees that the exercise by the Secretary-General of his managerial rights is legally and procedurally correct, and it protects the contractual and statutory rights of staff members of the United Nations.

This work is intended as a descriptive-analytical study of the function and jurisprudence of the Tribunal. More specifically, it attempts (1) to describe the Tribunal's theoretical underpinnings, historical background, structure, procedure, and practice; (2) to analyze and expound its jurisprudence in both quantitative and substantive terms; and (3) to make some tentative generalizations, on the basis of the above, about the Tribunal's uses and limits, as well as its legal and administrative implications.

This is a case study of a judicial organ in the contemporary international setting. It is neither a general treatise on international administrative tribunals nor an exhaustive exposition of the subject of legal protection of the international civil servant. Rather, it focuses on the procedure, law, and implications of one organ— the Tribunal.

The psychological and sociological dimensions of the subject remain unexplored. Questions such as "In what ways does the Tribunal contribute to the persistence of the United Nations Organization as a whole?" and "In what ways does it hamper the functioning of the Secretary-General?" are left largely unanswered, although the first question is the subject of some speculation.

These aspects can best be viewed in an empirical investigation combining the techniques of questionnaire, interview, and observation; however, due to the methodological difficulties involved, investigation of them was considered neither feasible nor desirable for the purposes of this study.

Although the Tribunal performs a patently useful function for the international civil service and has produced an interesting body of case-law, it has thus far attracted but scanty scholarly attention. Of the few studies on the subject, the most authentic and lucid is provided by a person most intimately acquainted with it, Mme. Paul Bastid, who has been a member of the Tribunal since its inception in 1950 and its president since 1953. In her scholarly lectures published in *Recueil des cours*,[2] she deals comprehensively with the various legal and procedural aspects of international administrative tribunals—of which the Tribunal is one. She combines the unique insights of a participant-observer and the mastery of her subject to produce what may justly be regarded as the best work yet on the general topic of international administrative tribunals. An article by Mme. Bastid on "Statut Juridique des Fonctionnaires des Nations Unies"[3] also deals with the Tribunal, albeit briefly, and serves as an excellent introduction to its work.

In *The Proper Law of International Organisations,* C. Wilfred Jenks, an experienced international lawyer and civil servant, probes the jurisprudence of the Tribunal in an attempt to "explore the impact of contemporary developments in international organisation on the borderlands of public international law, private international law and administrative law."[4] The general thesis of the book, in his own words, is that "the emergence of international body corporate has made it necessary to rethink the whole question of the law applicable to the legal status and transactions of such bodies."[5] He examines and expounds the principles and precedents governing the law applicable to the legal relations and transactions of international organizations not merely with their officials, employees, and agents but also with third parties. Like Mme. Bastid's lectures, Jenks's work does not confine itself to the Tribunal but draws freely upon the judgments of all international administrative tribunals. Of particular value is his comprehensive and authoritative exposition of the law applicable by such tribunals.

There have been other studies. In an article in *International Organization,* Wolfgang Friedmann and Arghyrios A. Fatouros examine the developing role of the Tribunal in international administration.[6] Theirs is an interesting and highly competent discussion of such topics as the theoretical background, history, composition and competence, procedure, and case-law of the Tribunal.

Some legal problems of the Tribunal are briefly but brilliantly discussed by Philip C. Jessup in his stimulating work, *Transnational Law.*[7] He deals mainly with the law applicable by the Tribunal, but his treatment also gives an excellent bird's-eye view of that body's function and jurisprudence. A description of the law and procedure of international administrative tribunals, including the Tribunal, is also found in Mohammed Bedjaoui's study of international civil service *Fonction Publique Internationale et influences Nationales* and Woonsang Choi's work on "The Legal Regulation of Employment Relations within International Organizations."[8]

These studies tend to throw a fair amount of light on the law and procedure of the Tribunal. However, while both Mme. Bastid's lectures and Jenks's volume are rather comprehensive, they are not exclusively concerned with the Tribunal. As a result, its case-law is not fully expounded. On the other hand, the article by Friedmann and Fatouros, while solely concerned with the Tribunal, is somewhat sketchy. It is a valuable guide to, but not a substitute for, a more detailed study. Likewise, the other works mentioned are not so much full-fledged studies related to the Tribunal, as introductions to its work.

This study, then, is intended to fill an obvious gap. Underlying it are some a priori considerations, of which two in particular must be made explicit:

1. International administration is here to stay. The United Nations—its main institutional expression—is likely to play an increasingly important role in the management of world affairs. This is not to say that the United Nations is a harbinger of world government. Nor is it the same as saying that the world organization, near universal in membership, is the solution or substitute for power politics among nations. Rather, the record of its two decades' existence suggests that the role this multination body can successfully play is an appreciably modest one. Its function as a pacemaker of the rule of law, as Herbert W. Briggs suggested more than a decade ago, is to provide a "framework to facilitate the development of the required 'social fabric' which in turn permits the establishment of the orderly processes of the rule of law." [9]

Its role as a regulator of naked force at the international level is cogently summarized by Inis L. Claude, Jr.:

Realistically, the potential usefulness of the United Nations in dealing with the dangers of international violence does not lie in the imposition of coercive restraint upon states determined to blow things up. It lies in the possibility of the Organization's helping states to avoid the creation or the exacerbation of situations which might produce explosions that none of them can want as long as national policies are controlled by rational men. [10]

In short, it is recognized that while the United Nations has its limitations, it is nevertheless a continuously useful organization, not merely for epitomizing mankind's eternal aspirations for a world ruled by law and peace but for helping to see that these aspirations are not shattered by what Hans J. Morgenthau calls "the self-defeating absurdity" [11] of a thermonuclear holocaust.

2. As in all administrative organizations, the flesh and bones of international administration are its personnel—the men and women who serve in the international secretariat. Hence, the success or

failure of the United Nations Organization is vitally dependent upon its ability to attract, maintain, and develop persons possessing, in the phraseology of the Charter, "the highest standards of efficiency, competence, and integrity." [12] Jurisdictional guarantees which the Tribunal affords the international civil servant, then, are one of the essential preconditions for the success of the Organization.

CHAPTER 1

THE U.N. PERSONNEL SYSTEM AND EMPLOYMENT SECURITY

THE UNITED NATIONS CHARTER designates the Secretary-General as "the chief administrative officer of the Organization" and further grants him the power to appoint the staff "under regulations established by the General Assembly." [1] The Staff Regulations, which spell out "the broad principles of personnel policy for the staffing and administration of the Secretariat," empower him to "provide and enforce such rules consistent with these provisions as he considers necessary." [2]

In short, these provisions invest the Secretary-General with authority to carry out the personnel function of the United Nations. In actual practice, the function is delegated to the Office of Personnel in the Secretariat. The Office, headed by the Director of Personnel, consists of (1) the Office of the Director, (2) Departmental Services, (3) Recruitment Services, and (4) Health Services. [3] The organs which play a principal role in making personnel policies in the General Assembly are the Fifth (Administrative and Budgetary) Committee [4] and the Advisory Committee on Administrative and Budgetary Questions. The latter, as its name implies, is a purely advisory body, however. In addition, the Secretary-General receives advice, directly or indirectly, from such organs as the International Civil Service Advisory Board, the Joint Appeals Board, the Special Advisory Board, the Appointment and Promotion Board, the Joint Disciplinary Committee, and the Joint Advisory Committee.

In brief, the Secretary-General is the key figure in the personnel administration of the Secretariat, but he must observe the broad principles and policies laid down by the General Assembly. He normally acts through the Office of Personnel, and is advised by a number of consultative and advisory bodies.

The need for a top-notch civil service transcends national boundaries; the hurdles that must be overcome to meet that need, however, are far more formidable at the international level. What are some of the stumbling blocks and what are the United Nations' formulae for overcoming them?

Two broad guidelines are prescribed by the Charter for selecting staff members of the Secretariat: (1) the necessity of securing the highest standards of efficiency, competence, and integrity and (2) the importance of recruiting the staff on as wide a geographical basis as possible.[5] In addition, the Staff Regulations provide:

> In accordance with the principles of the Charter, selection of staff members shall be made without distinction as to race, sex, or religion. So far as practicable, selection shall be made on a competitive basis.[6]

It quickly becomes apparent that the first two requirements are not easily reconcilable with each other, for a technically competent staff may not be geographically representative, and vice versa. The substantial difference which exists in the standards and quality of education in different countries is partly responsible for this phenomenon. The formula used for meeting the second requirement, i.e., geographical distribution, is a quota system. Under this system, which applies only to the professional staff and excludes the General Service (clerical and secretarial) personnel and posts requiring linguistic skills, each member state is allocated a quota equal to its percentage contribution plus or minus 25 percent.[7] Thus, as of August 31, 1961, the member states with the largest quota or "desirable range" were the United States (647–862), the U.S.S.R. (271–362), the United Kingdom (155–258), France (128–213), and China (100–166). The numbers of professional posts actually occupied by the nationals of these countries were as follows: the United States, 627; the U.S.S.R., 118; the United Kingdom, 242; France, 173; and China, 102. [8]

The quota system has been widely criticized on various grounds. A former staff member of the Secretariat, for example, argues that because a "fairly satisfactory national distribution of posts exists, logical future policy should emphasize a positive line of conduct rather than rely upon the rough guidance provided by the existence

of national 'quotas,'" adding: "the damage done by excessive defer-
ence to geographical representation goes beyond the morale and
efficiency of the Secretariat. At its worst, it becomes self-defeating,
both from the point of view of the UN and from that of its several
Member States." [9]

Another writer, Sydney D. Bailey, on the other hand, urges "pro-
gressively greater flexibility" in the application of the principle of
geographical distribution without abandoning the principle altogether. He asserts that the relevant factors to be considered in
arriving at more equitable quotas include population, the equality
of member states, and "the financial and other contribution of states
to those peace–keeping, refugee, and economic assistance activities
of the United Nations not covered by the regular budget." [10]

In recruiting its staff members, the United Nations relies on most
of the conventional methods employed by national governments
and private business firms. The Office of Personnel not only solicits
qualified candidates from time to time but continuously receives
unsolicited applications from would-be international civil servants
from all corners of the globe. It uses examinations for such posts
as translators, précis writers, bilingual secretaries, clerks, typists,
and stenographers. The difficulties involved in the use of examinations, however, are many and varied. How can standard tests be
prepared for people of widely heterogeneous educational and cultural backgrounds? In order to be entirely fair, as Richard Swift
points out, examinations should be set in the language of the candidate. In practice, the United Nations expects candidates to be
fluent in at least one of the five official languages—Chinese, English,
French, Russian, and Spanish—and sets examinations only in those
languages.[11]

Examinations, moreover, cannot adequately measure many of
the qualities required of an international civil servant.[12] The United
Nations therefore does not use them for recruiting its top–ranking
personnel—positions where, in Swift's view, "the candidate's tem-
perament and attitude toward international cooperation are just as
important as his technical competence." [13] For financial reasons,
examinations are seldom used to recruit young career staff members for junior professional posts. As Swift predicts, "the UN will
undoubtedly continue to select its senior professional officers on the
basis of their education, experience, and background, using inter-

views where possible, and recommendations and confidential reports, when available." [14]

The difficulty of recruitment is further compounded by the
decreasing attractiveness of international employment. Bailey comments:

. . . . the experience of seventeen years has not eliminated idealism [attached
to being an international civil servant], but some of the glamor has worn
off. Career prospects at the United Nations are not as good as they were.
. . . In spite of recent increases in the base scales, salaries are significantly
lower than in a number of national services, and it is possible to attract
specialists in some fields only by exceeding the normal salary scales. Staff
morale has tended to sag, particularly at times when the United Nations
Secretariat has been abused. Sudden changes of policy, leading to redun-
dancies, have caused some insecurity. Every appointment of an insufficiently
qualified person depresses the general standard and discourages the more
able people from accepting posts in the future.[15]

In addition, some governments, particularly those of the developing countries, have been reluctant to release nationals specifically
asked for by the United Nations for obvious reasons. Furthermore,
most posts in the Secretariat require specialists rather than gen-
eralists. Thus, while there is a small, persistent demand for statis-
ticians, demographers, agronomists, cartographers, and economists,
the demand for what Bailey calls "the adaptable man or woman
of general competence who can usually make a satisfactory career
in a national civil service" is extremely limited.[16]

These considerations tend to underscore the need for a more
dynamic recruitment policy—a policy which will ensure, in the
words of Bailey, "continuous contacts . . . between the Office of
Personnel and appropriate professional associations, academic institutions, and official and semi–official agencies." [17]

The United Nations' personnel system may be broadly described
as a mixed, open career system in that it has the characteristics
of an open career system, while, at the same time, utilizing temporary appointment. The Secretary-General, who has the exclusive
power to appoint staff members under the Staff Regulations and
the Charter, can award three types of contracts—temporary, permanent, and regular. Temporary appointments are of three kinds:
probationary, fixed-term, and indefinite.[18]

The probationary appointment is normally granted to persons
under the age of fifty years who are recruited for career service.

The period of probationary service is two years; however, in exceptional circumstances it may be reduced or extended for a maximum of one additional year. At the end of the probationary service the holder of probationary appointment must go either "up or out": he either receives a permanent or a regular appointment or is separated from the service.[19]

The fixed-term appointment is granted for a period not exceeding five years to persons recruited for service of prescribed duration, including persons temporarily seconded by national governments or institutions for service with the United Nations. It does not carry any expectancy of renewal or of conversion to any other type of appointment. The indefinite appointment, which like the fixed-term appointment does not carry any expectancy of conversion to any other type of appointment, is usually granted to persons specifically recruited for mission service or service with the Office of the High Commissioner for Refugees or any other agency or office of the United Nations as may be designated by the Secretary-General.[20]

The permanent appointment is intended for career international civil servants. It is granted to staff members who are holders of a probationary appointment and who, by their qualifications, performance, and conduct, have fully demonstrated their suitability as international civil servants and have shown that they meet the high standards of efficiency, competence, and integrity established in the Charter. The regular appointment is awarded to staff members in the General Service and Manual Worker categories who are holders of probationary appointments and have shown that they meet the high standards of efficiency, competence, and integrity. It is for an indefinite period and may last until retirement. Both permanent and regular appointments are subject to review at the end of the first five years.[21]

The Secretary-General makes his decision on the suitability of staff members for permanent or regular appointments on the basis of recommendations made jointly by the Office of Personnel and the department or office concerned. Such recommendations, however, must be reported to the Appointment and Promotion Board before submission to the Secretary-General.[22] It consists of ranking staff members, appointed by the Secretary-General in consultation with the Staff Council, including the Director or Deputy Director of Personnel who serves *ex-officio* as a nonvoting member.[23] The

Board advises the Secretary-General on the appointment, promotion, and review of staff members.

From the above it is clear that the Secretariat has the elements of both career and temporary services. What is more, the career system which it envisages is an *open* system: it permits lateral entry at all levels. Preference, however, is always given to promotions from within. Thus Staff Regulation 4.4 stipulates:

Subject to the provisions of Article 101, Paragraph 3, of the Charter [which establish the criteria for personnel selection], and *without prejudice to the recruitment at all levels,* the fullest regard shall be had, in filling vacancies, to the requisite qualifications and experience of persons already in the service of the United Nations . . . [Italics mine].

The staff of the Secretariat is divided into three broad categories: (1) the Principal Officer and Director Category; (2) the Professional Category; and (3) the General Service Category. The Professional Category consists of: Assistant Officer (P–1), Associate Officer (P–2), Second Officer (P–3), First Officer (P–4), and Senior Officer (P–5). The first category consists of Principal Officer (D–1) and Director (D–2). Immediately above Director comes Under-Secretary.[24] This classification scheme suggests a rank-in-person, as opposed to a rank-in-position, system. As in the uniformed military service, rank resides in a person, not in the position he holds. The Secretary-General is excluded from the above.[25]

According to the late Dag Hammarskjöld, former Secretary-General of the United Nations, there are three essential principles of an international civil service: (1) it must be international in composition; (2) it must have exclusively international responsibilities; and (3) it must be "solely an administrative organ, eschewing political judgments and actions." [26] We have already seen that the first principle is met by the United Nations. That the remaining two principles are equally observed is clear from the provisions in the Staff Regulations governing the service, conduct, and privileges of staff members. Thus Regulation 1.1 provides:

Members of the Secretariat are international civil servants. Their responsibilities are not national but exclusively international. By accepting appointment, they pledge themselves to discharge their functions and to regulate their conduct with the interests of the United Nations only in view.

Staff members are subject to the authority of the Secretary-General: they must comply with his instructions and are responsible to him in the exercise of their functions.[27] This means that they must neither seek nor accept instructions from any government or any other authority external to the Organization.[28] They are duty bound to "conduct themselves at all times in a manner befitting their status as international civil servants."[29] While they are not required to give up their national sentiments or their political and religious convictions, they must at all times strive to maintain the "reserve and tact incumbent upon them by reason of their international status."[30] They must not divulge to any person confidential information obtained in the course of their official business.[31] Nor can they accept any honor, decoration, favor, gift, or remuneration from a government or source external to the Organization without the approval of the Secretary-General. The only exception to this general rule is for honor and decoration for war service.[32]

Staff members are further expected to be politically neutral. While they may exercise the right to vote, they must refrain from engaging in any political activity which is inconsistent with or might reflect adversely upon the independence and impartiality required by their status as international civil servants.[33] A passive membership in a political party and the payment of normal financial contribution, however, are permitted; in case of doubt as to the interpretation and application of these provisions, the staff member must request a ruling from the Secretary-General.[34]

By virtue of Article 105 of the Charter, staff members enjoy "such privileges and immunities as are necessary for the independent exercise of their functions in connection with the Organization."[35] However, these privileges and immunities furnish no excuse to the staff members, who enjoy them, for nonperformance of their private obligations or failure to observe laws or police regulations. The Secretary-General has the power to waive these privileges and immunities when he considers it necessary to do so.[36]

In return for their services, staff members receive compensation in terms of salary, allowances, home leaves, and other benefits customarily enjoyed by employees everywhere.[37] Salaries, according to Swift, assume greater importance in the United Nations than in national civil services or private businesses because of the extreme paucity of promotional possibilities in the Secretariat.[38] For staff members in the Professional Category, salary ranges from $4,800 net [39] (Assistant Officer, Step I) to $13,100 net (Senior Officer, Step

X). The range for Principal Officer is $12,080–$14,530 net, while that for Director is $14,530–$15,520 net.[40]

In recognition of staff members' right to organize, the Staff Regulations provide for the establishment of a Staff Council. Elected by the staff, the Council serves the purpose of ensuring continuous contact between employees and the Secretary-General. It is entitled to make proposals to the Secretary-General for improvements in the situation of staff members, both as regards their conditions of work and their general conditions of life.[41] The Council in turn elects a Staff Committee composed of Council members. Through the Staff Committee, the Council is consulted on questions relating to welfare and administration, including policy on appointments, promotions, and terminations, and on salaries and allowances.[42] In addition, a Joint Advisory Committee is established by the Secretary-General with staff participation. It advises him regarding personnel policies and general questions of staff welfare and may also make to him proposals for amendment of the Staff Regulations and Rules.[43]

The Secretary-General has the exclusive authority to hire and fire staff members. However, he must always conform with principles and procedures set forth in the Staff Regulations and Rules. The Staff Regulations distinguish between the terms "termination" and "dismissal"; although both refer to the firing of personnel, the latter is used when disciplinary measures are involved.

The Secretary-General may terminate a holder of a permanent appointment on any of the following grounds: abolition or reduction of posts due to the necessities of the service; unsatisfactory services; reasons of health; failure to meet the highest standards of integrity required by the Charter; lack of suitability as shown by facts anterior to the appointment of the staff member concerned; in the interest of the good administration of the Organization. When integrity or suitability are questioned, the Secretary-General must first refer the matter to a Special Advisory Board appointed by him.[44]

The last ground, i.e., "in the interest of the good administration of the Organization," met with vigorous opposition during the debate in the Fifth Committee in 1953. At that time Secretary-General Hammarskjöld indicated that his main purpose in introducing the said ground was "not to stigmatize a staff member in controversial cases." Under the proposed provision, he argued, he could avoid citing lack of integrity or misconduct or unsatisfactory service as the reason for terminating a staff member, thereby protecting the latter's interest.[45] Strong objections, however, were voiced by a number of representatives who believed that the power granted was so broad as to render superfluous other provisions regarding termination. They pointed out that because the Secretary-General would be the sole judge of the requirements of good administration, contracts would be liable to termination by unilateral decision of one of the contracting parties. They were of the opinion that discretionary powers should not take the place of legal rights and that the adoption of the said provision would create a feeling of insecurity among the staff.[46]

Fixed-term appointments may be terminated by the Secretary-General prior to the expiration date for any of the reasons listed above or for such other reason as may be specified in the letter of appointment. The Secretary-General may at any time terminate probationary appointments, if in his opinion, such action would be in the interest of the United Nations.[47] Staff members whose appointments are terminated are paid an indemnity and repatriation grant when applicable.[48]

The Secretary-General has the power to impose disciplinary measures on staff members whose conduct is unsatisfactory and summarily to dismiss a staff member for serious misconduct.[49] Disciplinary measures consist of written censure, suspension without pay, demotion, and dismissal. Suspension pending investigation, however, is not considered as a disciplinary measure. Except in cases of summary dismissal, no staff member serving at the United Nations Headquarters in New York may be subject to disciplinary measure until the matter has been referred for advice to the Joint Disciplinary Committee, an advisory body consisting of a chairman selected by the Secretary-General in consultation with the Staff Committee, a member appointed by the Secretary-General, and a member elected by the staff. Referral to the Committee may be waived by mutual agreement of the staff member concerned and the Secretary-General.[50]

The two organs of major importance in safeguarding the rights of staff members are the Joint Appeals Board and the Administrative Tribunal. One provides administrative remedy, and the other legal remedy. The striking difference between the two is that whereas the Board is a purely advisory body, the Tribunal is a strictly judicial organ capable of pronouncing binding judgments. The Board nevertheless is closely linked with, and indispensable to, the operation of the Tribunal, for most disputes must first come to the Board before they may be admitted to the Tribunal. Furthermore, unlike the Tribunal which lacks competence in disciplinary cases, the Board can hear disputes involving disciplinary measures. In this respect, the Board may be regarded as complementing, as well as facilitating, the work of the Tribunal.

The main function of the Board is to advise the Secretary-General regarding appeals filed by staff members against an administrative decision alleging the nonobservance of their terms of appointment, including all pertinent regulations and rules, or against disciplinary action. In case of termination or other action on grounds of inefficiency or relative efficiency, the Board does not consider the substantive question of efficiency, but only evidence that the decision has been motivated by prejudice or by some other extraneous factor. Any dispute as to its competence is settled by the Board itself.[51]

The Board consists of three members: (1) a chairman selected from a panel appointed annually by the Secretary-General after consultation with the Staff Committee; (2) a member appointed annually by the Secretary-General; and (3) a member elected annually by ballot of the staff. In addition, alternates are selected in the same manner as the members; an alternate serves during the consideration of an appeal for which a member is unavailable or otherwise disqualified.[52] The first step for a staff member who wishes to appeal an administrative decision is to address a letter to the Secretary-General, requesting that the administrative decision be reviewed. Such a letter must be sent within one month from the time the staff member received notification of the decision in writing.[53]

In order to make an appeal against the answer received from the Secretary-General, the staff member must submit his appeal in writing to the Secretary of the Board within two weeks from the date of receipt of the answer. If no reply has been received from the Secretary-General within two weeks, he may still submit his appeal in writing to the Secretary of the Board within the two following weeks. The time limit of two weeks applies to an appeal against the Secretary-General's decision on disciplinary action. The staff member concerned must, within two weeks of the notification of the Secretary-General's decision, file such an appeal with the Secretary of the Board. The Board may waive the above time limits in exceptional circumstances.[54]

The staff member may be represented before the Board by another member of the Secretariat. The filing of an appeal with the Board does not have the effect of suspending the administrative decision contested. Proceedings before the Board are normally limited to the original written presentations of the case, together with brief statements and rebuttals, which may be made either orally or in writing. The Board, by majority vote, adopts and submits a report to the Secretary-General, normally within three weeks after undertaking consideration of an appeal. The final decision of the Secretary-General in the matter, together with the Board's recommendation, is communicated to the staff member. The Staff Committee is also supplied with the above information, except in cases of appeals against disciplinary action.[55]

The Tribunal stands as the final guardian of staff rights. When the staff member's complaint persists, he may bring the case before the Tribunal for final adjudication. The details regarding the law and procedure of such adjudication are examined in the remainder of the study.

In brief, the Secretary-General, who is the chief administrative officer of the Organization, is responsible for the personnel administration of the United Nations. In conformity with the mandate of the Charter, he must constantly strive to attract, maintain, and develop a competent and truly international staff. The personnel system has been previously described herein as a mixed, open career system. As international civil servants, staff members of the United Nations have unique duties and obligations: they have to be ever mindful of the collective interests of the world organization and to conduct themselves in a manner befitting their international status. They enjoy the corresponding rights, privileges, and benefits, including procedural guarantees against infringement of their legal rights.

As will become apparent in Chapter V, the majority of disputes that come before the Tribunal have their origin in the Secretary-General's decision to terminate appointments, both temporary and permanent. This, coupled with the fact that the authors of the Statute of the Tribunal were specifically motivated by their concern for employment security of staff members, strongly suggests that the Tribunal is, in effect, legal guardian of the employment security of the international civil servant.

It may be noted, in this connection, that Max Weber, widely recognized as the foremost authority in bureaucratic theory, specifically listed employment security as one of the structural imperatives of bureaucratic organization.[56] If one accepts Weber's thesis, then it is possible to regard the Tribunal as fulfilling an essential existential need of the larger structure of which it is a part—the United Nations Organization. In any event, it is worthwhile to examine briefly the problem of employment security, its meaning, and implications.

Employment security, it must be stressed, does not necessarily mean the guarantee of tenure for life. Nor does it promise absolute security of employment—that is, a guarantee against dismissal on any grounds whatsoever. It must be understood in a relative sense; as Weber pointed out, "where legal guarantees against arbitrary dismissal or transfer are developed, they merely serve to guarantee a strictly objective discharge of specific duties free from all personal considerations." [57]

It can easily be seen that there are two aspects of the problem: employment security as an objective fact and employment security as a subjective feeling. In different words, it is quite possible to conceive a situation in which a person may feel that his job is very insecure in spite of the fact that there exists in reality every institutional safeguard against arbitrary dismissal. The situation just described, however, must be regarded as an exception rather than the rule; we may therefore assume that the objective fact and the feelings of security are not necessarily antithetical but positively related. Thus understood, employment security is a tangible phenomenon identifiable by a number of operational indices.

According to Frederick Herzberg and his associates, these include "those features of the job situation which lead to assurance for continued employment, either within the same company or within the same type of work or profession." They add: "In some instances, this means that the opportunity for mobility is absent but continued employment is assured; in other cases, the immediate job continuation may not be as secure, but there are sufficient opportunities for immediate re-employment elsewhere that survival pressures and unstable labor demands arouse little or no anxiety in the worker." [58]

When it is confined to a single organizational context, employment security may be ascertained in terms of such criteria as: the stability of the organization concerned; specified grounds for dismissal; institutional mechanisms for reviewing alleged violations of employment rights; the effectiveness of the above mechanisms as shown by their actual performance; and the rate of personnel turnover. In short, employment security signifies a reasonable degree of assurance, embodied in an effective, formalized review procedure, that an employee's job will not arbitrarily be forfeited.

Research findings and opinions are divided as to the importance of employment security in determining the worker's attitude. An analysis of American and British experimental studies and attitude surveys led Morris S. Viteles to conclude in 1953 that lack of employment security had adverse effects on the attitude of some workers and little effect on others. He attributed the disparity of findings to the possibility that "difference in *intelligence,* as well as in occupational levels, affects attitudes towards economic security and the role of steady work as an incentive." He felt that there might be an inverse relationship between intelligence and occupational levels on the one hand and the desire for job security on the other.[59]

A similar conclusion was reached by Herzberg *et al* who had also found conflicting results in the findings of empirical research. In one group of studies they found that employment security consistently ranked as the most important factor affecting employee attitude and that "security is a strong reason for liking a job, but infrequently is this mentioned as the major reason for dissatisfactions." [60] On the other hand, the results of another study indicated that employment security was the least important of job attitude factors. The difference in occupational level, age, and education of the respondents was cited as the probable cause for the disparity of findings.[61]

An interesting argument is presented by a British social psychologist regarding employment security. Nigel Walker argues in his study of morale in the British civil service that security, or insecurity, to be more precise, of employment is an important motivator of workers.[62] He theorizes:

In almost every organization of full-time workers the most obvious incentive to work hard and efficiently is the fear of losing the job. There are of course certain conditions under which this fear is too remote to be effective. Among prisoners and military conscripts, for example, it disappears altogether. A shortage of skilled labour may deter an employer from sacking an idle craftsman, who may, in any case, know that he can find a similar job with ease. Or the employees may be organized into unions that can use the counter-threat of withdrawing their members from work in order to protect individuals against dismissal.[63]

Since none of these special conditions is present to an effective extent in the British nonindustrial civil service, Walker sees "no obvious reason why the threat of dismissal should not be an effective incentive" in it.[64]

In a study of the attitudes of American higher civil servants toward their career, Dwaine Marvick suggests that a reasonable guarantee of job security is a minimum reward expected by career-oriented civil servants. He asserts that the divergent interests of bureaucratic organization and its members can be reconciled, or satisfactorily adjusted, through professionalization, which requires that two conditions be met: (1) not only does an individual have to commit himself to a recognized career in the organization, (2) but he must feel that "the organization where he works is sponsoring his career development and is routinely providing those job conditions which are to him the current reward for his career commitment." [65]

A similar line of reasoning is seen in the writings of Peter M. Blau, who, after examining the conflict between personal and organizational goals in two governmental agencies and the attendant dysfunctional consequences, suggests five prerequisites of adjustive development, headed by a "minimum of employment security." Noting that "insecurity in the bureaucratic situation, where one's job hangs in the balance, breeds ritualistic adherence to the existing order," he argues:

Employment security engenders the psychological freedom of action that enables individuals to initiate adjustments, but it does not guarantee that these will further the objectives of the agency. Indeed, tenure may lead to private adaptations that are detrimental to the interest of the organization. To preclude this possibility, a professional orientation must prevail among officials. This involves a common identification with professional values and norms, which makes the process of attaining professional objectives a source of satisfaction.[66]

The above survey of research and opinion shows that, in spite of lack of unanimity, the weight of argument supports the tentative conclusion that some measure of employment security is a necessary condition for the efficient operation of bureaucratic organization. The absence of such security is liable to constrain its members to be capricious, subservient, rigid, and unimaginative (from the standpoint of the interests of the organization concerned)—in short, inefficient. Conversely, the effective guarantee of employment security is likely to stimulate their initiative and challenge their imagination, resulting in a fuller realization of both personal and organizational goals than is otherwise possible.

One theoretical question may be raised in connection with employment security: is employment security *always* desirable from either the organizational or individual point of view? In the absence of any conclusive empirical evidence one way or the other, no definite answer is possible now. Nevertheless, one may very well argue that the important question is not whether there should be employment security, but how much employment security and what kind. It is intuitively obvious that too much security is just as injurious to the healthy development of an organization as is too little. For only by bringing in new members from time to time and sending away those who have outlived their usefulness to the organization can it hope to maintain the freshness of outlook, the vitality of operation, and the ability to adapt itself to the constantly changing environment—to be fully alive, rather than partly stagnant.

To reiterate, some guarantee of employment security is theoretically essential to the functioning of bureaucracy. What is more, this concept is widely honored in practice. Thus, if we examine the practice of three leading national bureaucracies, namely the civil services of France, Great Britain, and the United States, we find that their civil servants enjoy marked, though varying, degrees of employment security. In France the *fonctionnaire* typically enjoys an effective guarantee of his employment rights, the most important of which is a reasonably secure career. He is protected by an elaborate administrative and legal machinery, culminating in the famous *Conseil d'Etat*.[67] In Great Britain we find that a high degree of employment security obtains in spite of a complete lack of clear-cut formal guarantees to that effect. In theory the British civil servant holds his office "at the Queen's pleasure" and may be dismissed at any time by her Minister. In reality he is seldom dismissed as long as he behaves himself and fulfills his functions in a responsible manner.[68]

The civil servant in the United States federal government has at his disposal both administrative and legal remedies against arbitrary dismissal. He has the right of appeal both within his agency and to the Civil Service Commission. In addition, he is fully entitled to take his case to the regular, as distinct from administrative, courts, there being no separate administrative tribunals in the United States. While the degree of security enjoyed by him is not as high as that granted to his French or British counterpart, the American civil servant nevertheless is sufficiently safeguarded from arbitrary action.[69]

All of this serves to underscore the point that some measure of employment security is both desirable and necessary for the efficient functioning of bureaucratic organization. The importance of the Tribunal in the overall effectiveness of the United Nations Organization may be more fully appreciated in this light.

THE BLUEPRINT

EVERY HUMAN INSTITUTION was created to serve specific purposes. To say this is not to imply that the original intentions and expectations of its creators necessarily materialize. It is not only useful but essential to place an institution in its proper historical perspective if we are to intelligently comprehend its present form and functioning.

The Administrative Tribunal of the United Nations is a direct lineal descendant, in a spiritual sense, of the Administrative Tribunal of the League of Nations. And though the League Tribunal provides a point of departure for our brief historical survey, an examination of the theoretical basis of international administrative tribunals seems a necessary preliminary step.

The importance of a formalized mechanism which safeguards the rights and security of employees in bureaucratic organization has already been demonstrated. The rationale for administrative tribunals in general is to be found, finally, in the operational needs of a large-scale administrative organization. If such an organization is to function properly—that is to say, if its administration is to be flexible, realistic, and responsive, not only to organizational but to situational needs—then the administrator must necessarily be vested with a wide range of discretionary powers.

The fact that the administrator thus possesses discretionary authority necessitates some kind of control mechanism. For no human being is infallible; unbridled power, of necessity, is open to abuse. Moreover, no employee will long tolerate either infringement of his rights or subjection to arbitrary authority. What kinds

24

of control mechanism, then, stand ready for use? There are two such mechanisms: hierarchical and judicial controls. Under the former, the actions of the administrator are subject to the surveillance of his hierarchical superior, if such a superior exists. Employees whose rights have been infringed have a right of appeal to the supreme administrative officer of the organization concerned. The latter's decisions are considered final and without appeal. Judicial control, on the other hand, refers to a system under which an impartial body adjudicates any dispute arising between the administrator and employees.

The disadvantages of the first method, i.e., hierarchical control, are readily apparent. It makes the administrator a judge in his own case. Aside from the possibility that there may be no hierarchical superior to appeal to, except the very administrator whose decision is contested, there is a very real danger that the superior will be biased in favor of his subordinate administrator who has made the decision in dispute. As Friedmann and Fatouros speculate:

> The mere existence of such a possibility tends to make the subordinate [the rank-and-file employee] feel dependent on his superior's whims and thus to divert his attention from service to personal considerations. An atmosphere of distrust is created, every official resenting the favors that he thinks are shown to others, and a permanent sense of insecurity prevails in the service, which does not let the officials devote themselves exclusively to their duties.[1]

For these reasons, the second method, i.e., judicial control, is more widely utilized in actual practice. Such a control usually manifests itself institutionally in the form of administrative tribunals. The organization, role, and "dignity" of such tribunals, however, vary considerably depending upon the particular system of law to which they have reference.[2] Thus, whereas France has a well-developed system of administrative tribunals culminating in the *Conseil d'Etat*, no separate administrative courts exist in Britain and the United States. In Britain the recourse to regular courts for settlement of administrative disputes is seriously limited by what Mme. Bastid calls "la règle de l'irresponsibilité de la Couronne en matière quasi–delictuelle et le principe suivant lequel la Couronne peut révoquer le *civil servant* 'at its pleasure'."[3] In the United States regular courts can decide civil service disputes.

The above theoretical considerations are equally germane in the international realm. For international organizations, too, are confronted with the same administrative necessity for efficient functioning, and thus for administrative discretion on the one hand, and for keeping such discretion within bounds on the other. However, there is an additional factor which points toward the theoretical justifiability as well as the practical wisdom of creating international administrative tribunals. It is the special and unique position of international organizations, namely, their *international* nature. They are explicitly designed to serve, not a particular state or group of states, but the international community, i.e., the world at large.[4] Their international staff neither seeks nor receives instructions from any individual country. In short, international organizations operate independently of national control and pressures.

From this it follows that an international organization cannot be subject to the jurisdiction of any national court. It is logically necessary therefore that there should exist an international court having jurisdiction over international organizations. The present International Court of Justice, however, enjoys only an advisory jurisdiction over international organizations. In contentious cases, *only states* can be parties before the Court.[5] Neither does the individual have a *locus standi* before the Court. Hence the need for international tribunals which are specifically empowered to deal with disputes arising out of employment relations in international organizations.

In short, the need for international administrative tribunals arises from what Mme. Bastid terms *"la vie administrative des organizations internationales."* [6] In the words of Manley O. Hudson, "The interpretation and application of contracts of service required an exercise of the judicial function, and as the organizations themselves were not subject to the jurisdiction of any national courts, need arose for vesting competence in special international tribunals." [7]

The progenitor of international administrative tribunals is to be found in the League of Nations. Not only has the League Tribunal served as a model for similar tribunals established elsewhere, but it has also effectively survived the League of Nations itself. It continued its existence under the roof of the International Labour Office.[8]

In the early days of the League the only guarantee against arbitrary action granted to the international civil servant was the right of appeal in cases of dismissal. However, as already noted, such a hierarchical recourse has serious inherent limitations. Doubts soon began to be expressed as to the value of such a procedure; Albert Thomas, then director of the International Labour Office, was led to declare in 1921 that it was necessary to set up a judicial organ "qui remplirait un rôle analogue à celui du Conseil d'Etat en France." [9]

Despite the foresighted suggestions of Thomas, however, it remained for the so-called Monod case to dramatize the urgency of the need for such a legal mechanism. In 1925 François Monod, a former staff member of the League, appealed to the League Council for damages on the ground that his arbitrary dismissal by the Secretary-General constituted a breach of contract. The Council then invited the Supervisory Commission to conduct an inquiry into the matter. The latter in turn recommended that the dispute be referred to an ad hoc Commission of Jurists, to be appointed by the Council. [10]

The Commission, composed of three eminent jurists, [11] unanimously decided in favor of the complainant, recommending an award of compensation equivalent to his nine months' salary. The recommendation was subsequently carried out. In its advisory opinion, the Commission touched on an important question, i.e., the nature of the legal tie between the Secretary-General and the complainant. Such a relationship, it held, could not be judged according to the principles of private law and civil laws but must be regulated, above all, by "les principes de droit public et des lois administratives." [12]

In 1925 the Supervisory Commission asked one of its members, M. Nederbrgt, to conduct a preparatory study on "la création éventuelle d'une instance à laquelle le personnel de la S.d.N. pourrait faire appel au cas òu il estimerait ses droits et ses intérêts injustement lèsés." [13] Out of this study grew a blueprint for an Administrative Tribunal of the League of Nations. Its salient features included the following:

1. The proposed Tribunal would be a judicial body designed to afford the staff member a sense of security emanating from justice;

2. It would provide "a judge for every case" and would "prevent one party from being a judge in his own case";

3. Its judgments would be final and without appeal. [14] In addi-

tion, it specifically emphasized that such a Tribunal would rein-force, rather than reduce, the authority of the administration.

After a considerable debate and a series of draft statutes, the Assembly of the League finally adopted the proposal on September 20, 1927. However, it took the action on a trial basis; it reserved the right to modify or abolish the Tribunal on the basis of a 3-year experience. At the same time, the procedure for an appeal to the Council or to the International Labour Office was abrogated.[15]

On December 9, 1927, the Council, in accordance with the provisions of the Statute of the newly established Tribunal, appointed three judges and three deputy–judges to the Tribunal. The newly appointed judges were Devèze (Belgium), Froelich (Germany), and Montagna (Italy). The deputy judges were De Tomcsanyi (Hungary), Eide (Denmark), and van Ryckerversel (Holland). The members of the Tribunal were to be remunerated in terms of per diem allowance. The Tribunal would be competent to adjudicate disputes arising out of alleged violations of contracts of service or of staff regulations. Access to the Tribunal was given to officials or ex-officials of the League Secretariat or of the International Labour Office and to their successors in interest. The competence *ratione personae* was later extended to officials of the Institute of Intellectual Cooperation, the International Educational Cinematographic Institute, and the Nansen International Office for Refugees. In 1931 the Assembly confirmed the Statute without amendment.[16]

In its eighteen years of existence, from 1928 to 1946, the League Tribunal passed thirty-seven judgments. At the end of 1939 it had decided fifteen applications against the Secretary-General, four against the I.L.O., one against the Administrative Board of the Pension Fund (*le Conseil d'administration de la caisse des pensions*), and one against the Nansen International Office for Refugees. In 1946 it rendered sixteen judgments, two of which concerned the I.L.O.[17]

The questions with which the Tribunal was asked to deal were not so diverse; oftentimes several applications concerned the same subject, such as pensions (Judgments 1, 2, and 3), or the conditions under which a member of the Secretariat could be considered as not having been locally recruited (Judgments 5 to 12). Judgments 24 to 37, rendered on February 26, 1946, however,

precipitated a grave crisis. The Tribunal had ruled in these judgments that the acquired contractual rights of certain staff members
could not be affected by a resolution of the Assembly. The latter
disagreed, refusing to appropriate the funds necessary for implementing the above judgments.[18]

To be more specific, the dispute had its origin in the Assembly's
decision on December 14, 1939, to reduce the number of posts
in both the Secretariat and the I.L.O. in an effort to alleviate the
difficult financial situation which followed the outbreak of World
War II. A number of staff members refused to resign or accept the
suspension of their contracts on the ground that such actions constituted a breach of their contracts. Thirteen of them brought the
case before the Tribunal. In judgments rendered on February 26,
1946, the Tribunal ruled that the applications were well founded.
It ruled that it was wrong (à tort) for the Secretary-General to
apply the Staff Regulations as revised in 1939, because the contracts
of the applicants did not contain any clause indicating that the
Assembly had the authority to modify the Regulations. Hence
the Regulations in force at the time of the conclusion of the contracts were still applicable without modification in the absence of
mutual agreement to the contrary. In brief, the Tribunal declared
that the Assembly could not lawfully affect the acquired rights
of the staff members. The Assembly, as noted, responded by
imposing a financial veto on the judgments.[19]

This posed an important legal question. Can the Assembly lawfully refuse to carry out the judgments of the Tribunal? The problem was hotly debated in the Assembly, in particular in the Second
Committee which was charged with financial questions. A subcommittee report prepared by an eminent British jurist, Sir Hartley
Shawcross, contained the following majority opinions:

1. The Tribunal is not competent to question the validity of a
resolution adopted by the Assembly, such as the resolution of
December 14, 1939. It is under obligation only to give effect to that
resolution.

2. The interpretation given by the Tribunal to the effect that certain members are exempted from the consequences of that resolution
is erroneous.

3. The Assembly can lawfully declare by a legislative resolution
that the judgments rendered by the Tribunal are null and void,

not merely because the Tribunal bypassed the legislative act of the Assembly but also because of its erroneous conclusion concerning the intention of that act.[20]

The above views were vigorously criticized by a number of delegates, notably the eminent Belgian and Dutch jurists Kaeckenbeeck and Francois. They argued that the Tribunal had been vested with the power of interpretation and that, consequently, its interpretations must be respected. The refusal to execute the Tribunal's judgments, they maintained, encroached upon its authority and sovereignty. Furthermore, the Assembly had no legislative authority over the staff members whose legal tie with the League was based solely on their contracts. Despite these objections the report of the subcommittee was finally adopted by the Assembly by a vote of 16 to 8 with 4 abstentions; thus the Assembly's decision not to give effect to the judgments in question was reaffirmed.[21]

Kaeckenbeeck then presented a formal reservation on behalf of seven governments expressing the regret that the League should have refused to execute judgments duly pronounced by a tribunal which it had itself created when there was no pressing need to do so. The significance of this episode lay in the fact that "L'Assemblée, organe politique, refusait l'execution en invoquant des considérations juridiques, jouant ainsi, en fait, un rôle analogue a celui d'une instance de recours." [22]

When the League formally dissolved itself by a resolution of April 18, 1946, it was decided to maintain the Tribunal under a new name—the Administrative Tribunal of the International Labour Office. The Tribunal preserved its competence over staff members of the League Secretariat until October 31, 1946, for the benefit of those whose appointments were formally terminated on July 31, 1946. In fact, three cases were submitted on this basis, and the judgments thereon were handed down in February, 1947. This brought an end to the functioning of the Tribunal as a League organ.[23]

In brief, while the League Tribunal "did not establish an extensive body of case-law," [24] it nevertheless made a significant contribution to the development both of the international civil service and of international administrative tribunals. It was the first, and on the whole successful, experiment in legal protection of the rights of the international civil servant. As such it was to serve as a model for future international administrative tribunals.

The moderately successful operation of the League Tribunal aroused considerable interest among other international organizations. Thus in 1929 the International Institute of Agriculture sought to establish a similar tribunal on the League's pattern. The Italian Court of Cassation suggested in 1931 that, since the Institute enjoyed immunity from Italian jurisdiction, it could profitably create an administrative tribunal of its own, competent to deal with complaints by its staff members. Accordingly, in 1932 the General Assembly of the Institute adopted a statute relating to the adjustment of disputes which provided, *inter alia*, for an ad hoc administrative tribunal in each case. However, no such tribunal was actually set up to deal with any dispute in the subsequent years.[25]

It was already noted that the Administrative Tribunal of the I.L.O. is a successor to the League Tribunal. Until the dissolution of the League in 1946, the staff members of the I.L.O. were under the jurisdiction of the League Tribunal. When the juridical basis of the Tribunal was changed as a result of the resolution of the League Assembly on April 18, 1946, the I.L.O. personnel, together with the soon-to-be separated staff members of the League Secretariat, came under the jurisdiction of the I.L.O. Tribunal. The changeover, which also entailed some revision of the Tribunal's Statute, was confirmed by the Governing Body (*le Conseil d'administration*) of the I.L.O. on May 27, 1946. In the following year the General Conference of the Organization officially approved the revised Statute.[26]

An important addition to the Statute was the provision for an advisory opinion from the International Court of Justice in cases where the Governing Body of the I.L.O. or the Administrative Board of the Pension Fund should challenge the jurisdiction of the Tribunal or should consider that a decision of the Tribunal was vitiated by a fundamental fault in procedure. The opinion given by the Court would be binding.[27] A later amendment to the Statute stipulated that other intergovernmental international organizations could accept the jurisdiction of the Tribunal with respect to disputes between them and their staff members, provided that the prescribed procedures were followed for such acceptance. A number of organizations have since taken advantage of this provision and are now under the jurisdiction of the Tribunal. These include the F.A.O. (Food and Agriculture Organization), W.H.O. (World Health Organization), UNESCO (United Nations Educational Scientific and Cultural Organization), I.T.U. (International Telecommunication Organization), and W.M.O. (World Meteorological Organization).[28]

The Tribunal is competent to deal with (1) complaints of staff members alleging nonobservance, in substance or form, of the terms of appointment or of applicable staff regulations; (2) disputes concerning compensation in cases of invalidity, injury, or disease incurred in the course of employment; and (3) complaints on nonobservance of the Staff Pension Regulations. As was the case with its predecessor, the Tribunal is composed of three judges and three deputy judges of different nationalities. They are appointed by the I.L.O. Conference for a period of three years. Three members, at least one of whom must be a judge, constitute a quorum. Staff members must have exhausted all the administrative remedy available before complaints may be filed.[29]

As of August, 1960, the Tribunal had rendered thirty-nine judgments.[30] Of special interest is the fact that the competence of the Tribunal was once challenged by the Executive Board of the UNESCO, which eventually requested an advisory opinion of the International Court of Justice on the matter. The Court, in its advisory opinion of October 23, 1956, confirmed the Tribunal's competence to hear the cases in question and upheld the validity of the judgments handed down by it. The Court said in part that "the circumstances that the Tribunal may have rightly or wrongly interpreted and applied the law for the purposes of determining the merits in no way affects its jurisdiction." [31]

The Tribunal continues to function today, and is one of the two major international administrative tribunals in existence, the other being the United Nations Tribunal.

The Organization for European Economic Cooperation, in accordance with Article 20 of its Staff Regulations adopted on April 17, 1948, has established an Appeals Board (*Commission de Recourse*) charged with adjusting disputes related to its functionaries. Unlike the Joint Appeals Board of the United Nations, which is an advisory body, the Board is competent to pronounce binding decisions on the basis of law. It may therefore be considered on a par with other international administrative tribunals.[32]

The Board is composed of two members, one representing the

Secretary-General of the Organization and another selected by the staff, and a chairman who represents the Council of the Organization. Proceedings before the Board are not open to public and information pertaining thereto is kept confidential.[33] As of August, 1960, it had rendered thirty judgments dealing with a wide variety of questions; the points of law touched upon by the Board are also of considerable interest.[34]

The Institute of Rome for the unification of private law had originally accepted the jurisdiction of the League Tribunal. When Italy withdrew from the League, however, the Institute had to reorganize itself. Its new statute which entered force on April 21, 1940, envisaged a union of states. In 1952 the statute was amended to provide for the creation of an Administrative Tribunal. Due to lack of the required ratification, however, the amendment has not yet come into force.[35]

It is apparent from the above examples of international administrative tribunals that the need for a judicial mechanism competent to adjust employment disputes is inherent in international organizations or, more specifically, in what Mme. Bastid calls the "fonctionnement de l'entreprise administrative internationale." [36] Small wonder, then, that the United Nations soon felt the same need and proceeded to establish an Administrative Tribunal of its own.

Although the idea of creating an Administrative Tribunal of the United Nations was first entertained by the Preparatory Commission as early as 1945, it did not come to fruition until late 1949. A survey of the problems encountered and points raised in the course of its establishment is indispensable to a fuller understanding of the Tribunal.

The Preparatory Commission of the United Nations foresaw the need for an Administrative Tribunal. Its Executive Committee recommended on November 12, 1945, that early consideration should be given to the advisability of establishing an Administrative Tribunal to adjudicate on any complaint lodged against the Organization by an official in connection with the fulfillment of the terms of his contract. Such a Tribunal, it said, would be modeled on the League Tribunal.[37]

The Sub–Committee on Staff Regulations likewise proposed:

An Administrative Tribunal should be established at an early date. It should be competent to adjudicate any dispute arising in connection with the fulfilment of an official's contract. The Secretary-General should be authorized to appoint a small advisory committee, possibly including representatives of the Staff, to draft a statute for the Administrative Tribunal for submission to the Assembly. The Tribunal might include an expert on relations between employers and employed in addition to jurists.[38]

Underlying the above proposals was the view that some measure of employment security and the guarantee thereof were prerequisite to the fostering of a competent international civil service. Specifically, it was reasoned that unless members of the staff could be offered some assurance of being able to make their careers in the Secretariat, many of the best candidates would inevitably be kept away. Further, members of the staff could not be expected fully to subordinate the interests of their countries to the international interest if they were merely detached temporarily from national services and remained dependent upon them for their future prospects. Finally, it was considered important that the advantages of experience should be secured within the Secretariat, and sound administrative traditions established. These doubtless called for a relatively permanent staff, which in turn required adequate safeguards for the rights and security of the staff.[39]

In compliance with the recommendations of the Preparatory Commission, the General Assembly on February 13, 1946, adopted a resolution authorizing the Secretary-General "to appoint a small advisory committee, possibly including representatives of the staff, to draft for submission to the Second Part of the First Session of the General Assembly a statute for an administrative tribunal." Pursuant to that resolution, the Secretary-General set up an advisory committee for the suggested purpose.[40]

Headed by Thanassis Aghnides, then Ambassador of Greece in London and formerly Under-Secretary-General of the League of Nations, the Committee had the following members: Manley O. Hudson, formerly judge of the Permanent Court of International Justice; Joseph Nisot, Counsellor of the Belgian Embassy in Washington, alternate representative of Belgium on the Economic and Social Council, formerly the member of the Legal Section of the Secretariat of the League of Nations who acted as Registrar of the Administrative Tribunal of the League; Ladislar Radimsky, deputy of the Czechoslovak representative to the United Nations; Jean Herbert (chairman of the Permanent Staff Committee), member of the Secretariat; with Frank Begley (member of the Permanent

Staff Committee), member of the Secretariat, as alternate; M. Perez-Guerrero, member of the Secretariat; with J. G. Stewart, member of the Secretariat, as alternate; Marc Schreiber (member of the Permanent Staff Committee), member of the Secretariat; with E. Ranshofen-Wertheimer (member of the Permanent Staff Committee), member of the Secretariat, as alternate; and Mrs. Isobel Wallace, member of the Secretariat. In addition, David M. Levitan, of the Secretariat, served as secretary and technical consultant to the Committee.[41]

The Committee held a series of ten meetings at Lake Success from September 16 to 26, 1946, and worked out a draft statute of an Administrative Tribunal. In carrying out its assignment, the Committee was guided by the intentions of the Preparatory Commission as to the nature of the proposed Tribunal: The Tribunal would deal "only with questions of the interpretation of an official's contract and with the claims of officials for non-observance of the contract, and not with matters of internal administration which would go before internal bodies within the Secretariat and in which the Secretary-General's decision would be final." In addition, it held two objectives, namely, a simple organization and an expeditious procedure.[42]

The Committee also sought to take full advantage of the experience of previous international administrative tribunals, notably the Administrative Tribunals of the League and of the International Labour Office. However, it foresaw that a United Nations Tribunal would probably be more frequently resorted to, since the staff of the United Nations would be much more numerous than the staffs of the League and the I.L.O.[43]

The draft statute prepared by the Committee consisted of twelve articles. It provided, *inter alia*, that: "The Tribunal shall be competent to adjudicate upon applications alleging non–observance of contracts of employment of officials of the Secretariat of the United Nations or of the Registry of the International Court of Justice, including the pertinent provisions of staff regulations." (Art. 2) The term "staff regulations" was used in a generic sense: it was intended to cover generally rules and regulations relating to officials' contractual rights, including their rights to pensions. The Tribunal would be open to two broad classes of persons: officials as well as persons succeeding to their rights after their death, and other persons who might be entitled to rights under contracts of deceased officials including pertinent staff regulations. The Tribunal would have an exclusive competence to decide in any dispute as to its competence.[44]

It was understood that the proposed Tribunal would not interfere in matters relating to the conduct of administration within the discretion of the Secretary-General. Also envisioned was the establishment of other procedures for dealing in a preliminary way with complaints which officials might advance. Further, the Tribunal would not be a negotiating body; it would confine its activity to adjudication.[45]

In terms of composition, the Tribunal would have seven judges of different nationalities, to be selected with due regard for equitable geographical representation. Only three, however, would sit in any particular case. The method of recruiting the judges drew lengthy considerations from the Committee. While the primary quality of the judges should be "a judicial attitude of mind," it did not seem essential that all of them should have previous experience as judges or as juri-consults. To underscore the judicial character of the Tribunal, however, the majority of the members preferred an election by the International Court of Justice, "the principal judicial organ of the United Nations," to that by the General Assembly. An election would be held each year, and the judges, in office for three years, would be eligible for reelection.[46]

The place at which sessions would be held was left to the Tribunal to decide. The dates of ordinary sessions would be fixed by the Rules of the Tribunal. The president would have authority to convoke extraordinary sessions when required. The expenses of the Tribunal would be borne by the United Nations. It was envisaged that the compensation of the judges might take the form of daily allowances for their attendance. The details regarding the procedures of the Tribunal would be laid down in the Rules, to be established by the Tribunal.[47]

An application to the Tribunal would not be receivable "unless the decision contested was final and unless the person concerned has exhausted the means of redress available to him under applicable staff regulations." (Art. 7) With few exceptions, there would be a time limit of ninety days on the filing of applications. The filing of an application would not have the effect of suspending the execution of the decision contested.[48]

An interesting provision was the requirement that an applicant should deposit a sum of money within sixty days after filing his application. The underlying rationale was that it would "prevent burdening the Tribunal with frivolous claims." The deposited sum would be refunded at the time of judgment unless the Tribunal found that the application was frivolous.[49] The Tribunal would hold both written and oral proceedings. The extent to which the latter would be open to public was left to the Tribunal to decide in each case, as indicated in Article 9.

As to the remedy available to the applicant, the draft statute stipulated:

> If the Tribunal finds that the application is well founded, it shall order the rescinding of the decision contested or the specific performance of the obligation invoked; but if such rescinding or specific performance is impossible or inadvisable, the Tribunal shall order the payment to the applicant of compensation for the injury sustained. The compensation awarded shall be paid by the United Nations.[50]

The Tribunal would take all decisions by a majority vote, and the judgments would be final and without appeal. It was envisaged that the competence of the Tribunal might be extended to any specialized agency brought into relationship with the United Nations in accordance with the provisions of the Charter. This would be done upon the terms established by a special agreement to be made with each such agency by the Secretary-General.[51]

In submitting the draft statute containing the above provisions, the Committee was hopeful, in view of the "success of the League of Nations Administrative Tribunal," that the proposed Tribunal would be "a useful body for safeguarding harmony between the United Nations and its officials." It further noted:

> Without in any way embarrassing the authorities responsible for the conduct of administration, [the Tribunal] would give assurance to officials as to the protection of their contractual rights. The United Nations is not suable in any national court without its consent; nor can it be sued by an official in the International Court of Justice. By creating a tribunal to serve as a jurisdiction open to its many officials of various nationalities, the United Nations will be acting not only in the interest of efficient administration, but also in the cause of justice.[52]

The commendable work of the Committee notwithstanding, no action was forthcoming in the General Assembly. Upon the recommendation of a Joint Sub-Committee of the Fifth and Sixth Committees, it was decided to shelve the question until the next session of the General Assembly so as to allow more time for detailed examination of the question.[53]

It was not until the fourth session of the General Assembly that the question of actually setting up an Administrative Tribunal became a topic for serious discussion. In the meantime, Secretary-General Trygve Lie had established, as an interim measure, an Appeals Board composed of an impartial chairman and representatives both of the Secretary-General and the staff. On the basis of appraisal of that experience and of consultations with both the specialized agencies and the Staff Committee, the Secretary-General submitted on September 2, 1949, a draft resolution incorporating a revised statute for a United Nations Administrative Tribunal for the consideration of the General Assembly.[54] To this were added a memorandum of the Staff Committee, a report of the Advisory Committee on Administrative and Budgetary Questions, and a few other communications.

The Secretary-General took note of the fact that the Staff Association and a substantial number of specialized agencies favored the creation of an Administrative Tribunal. The Staff Association in a resolution passed on March 8, 1949, expressed a "strong desire" that such a Tribunal should be created. Similarly, the I.L.O., UNESCO, F.A.O., and W.H.O. had voiced their support in principle of the creation of an administrative tribunal. The International Bank for Reconstruction and Development and the International Monetary Fund, however, did not intend to participate in any Administrative Tribunal which might be established by the United Nations.[55]

Secretary-General Lie proposed a number of revisions to the draft statute. First of all, he wanted to restrict the Tribunal's competence *ratione temporis* so that it could not deal with any applications where the cause of complaint arose prior to January 1, 1950. Second, he intended to make it clear in Article 10 that the Secretary-General should decide whether it was impossible or inadvisable to rescind a previous decision or invoke a specific performance. This, he felt, should be an administrative, rather than a judicial, decision. Besides, he argued, only the Secretary-General was in a position to make such a decision. When the Secretary-General's decision was in the affirmative, compensation for the injuries sustained should be fixed by the Tribunal and paid by the United Nations. Finally, he proposed to add another article to make it plain that the statute might be amended by the General Assembly or such other organ of the United Nations as the General Assembly might designate.[56]

Regarding his discretionary authority, Lie pointed out that there were three areas of decision in which the Secretary-General's judgment should be final: (1) a decision as to whether a particular staff member's services are satisfactory or unsatisfactory, (2) the decision of fact in disciplinary cases where nonobservance of the terms of the staff member's appointment cannot reasonably be alleged, and (3) decisions of fact in cases of serious misconduct. He cited as the legal basis for the above authority the Provisional Staff Regulations 19 and 21. He further referred to the provision in the Charter which designated him Chief Administrative Officer of the Organization. His responsibility under this provision, he argued, could be satisfactorily discharged only if his judgment on the facts in the cases indicated above was considered final. He warned against the difficulty which would arise "if an independent Administrative Tribunal were given authority to reconsider the facts in such cases, in the absence of any reasonable allegation that the terms of an appointment had been violated, and reverse the decision of the Secretary-General." [57]

The response of the Staff Association, as noted, had always been favorable; it had passed, at various times, resolutions expressing its urgent desire for the establishment of an Administrative Tribunal. With regard to the Secretary-General's proposed amendments to the draft statute, it had three specific observations to make.

First, the Staff Committee entertained the view that the Tribunal should be competent to pass judgments not only on applications alleging nonobservance of contracts of employment of staff members, but also on applications concerning disciplinary action taken in respect of them. Disagreeing with the Secretary-General's view that this would interfere with his administrative responsibility and would further require an amendment of the Charter, the Staff Committee asserted that to grant employees a right to contest in the court disciplinary measures taken by employers was in keeping with accepted practice in most countries and would not constitute a transfer of power now vested in the Secretary-General. Moreover,

as the contractual relationship between the Organization and staff members is governed by the terms of their appointment *and* the regulations and rules, and as disciplinary measures are referred to both in the regulations and in the rules, any allegation of irregularity or inequity in the taking of disciplinary action actually is an allegation of non-observance of the contract of employment.[58]

Second, the Staff Committee was of the opinion that the Appeals Board should be retained when the Administrative Tribunal was established. Appreciative of the services rendered to it by the Board, the Staff Committee felt that the continued functioning of the Board would tend to reduce the number of cases brought before the Tribunal. It said:

The Staff Committee feels that the Tribunal should not have to deal with petty cases and, moreover, the consideration that the Tribunal would have to hear and pass judgment on a limited number of more important cases would be an inducement for eminent people to accept election as members of the Tribunal. Finally the Appeals Board would perform the highly useful function of preparing the case: the cases are investigated by the Appeals Board with a conscientiousness and thoroughness to which everybody pays tribute; its continuance would therefore facilitate the task of the Tribunal.[59]

In this connection, the Staff Committee proposed the deletion of Article 8 of the draft which provided for the deposit of a sum of money by staff members prior to filing their applications with the Tribunal. Why, it asked, should a staff member be suspected of making an unfounded claim? "Why should a serious litigant be deprived for months of a sum representing one week's salary?" It further noted that this requirement would be less onerous for relatively affluent staff members and thus indirectly it introduced inequality in the conditions on which the Tribunal would be open to staff members.[60]

Finally, the Staff Committee proposed to authorize the Tribunal to give advisory opinions. This, in its view, would serve to co-ordinate the functioning of the Appeals Board and the Tribunal. In addition, it was desirable both for the Secretary-General and for the staff that in case of doubt, the texts governing the relations between the Administration and staff members could be interpreted by a judicial authority.[61]

Aside from the above observations, the Staff Committee also voiced its views on "some points of less importance." It indicated that, in regard to Article 10, it would be in the interest both of the Secretary-General and the staff, if the Tribunal also should have a voice in the decision whether it was impossible or inadvisable to rescind an administrative decision or carry out the specific performance of an obligation. This, it felt, would assure that the Secretary-General would be supported by the Tribunal in a decision always of a delicate character, while the staff could rest assured that a decision on the matter would also be given by the highest judicial authority. The Staff Committee also requested that "compensation" be replaced by "full compensation." It stated:

> Full compensation should not only make up for financial losses, but also for loss in a reputation and any other loss suffered by the applicant. It is, of course, understood that full compensation instead of the rescinding of the contested decision or specific performance should only be applied in very exceptional circumstances.[62]

The Advisory Committee on Administrative and Budgetary Questions on September 28, 1949, submitted a report to the Fifth Committee regarding the administrative and budgetary consequences of the proposal to establish an Administrative Tribunal. The Committee indicated that it favored election of the members of the Tribunal by the General Assembly, rather than by the International Court of Justice. It also saw a need for redrafting Articles 10 and 13 so as to "ensure that any award made by the Tribunal to a staff member of a participating agency shall be the financial responsibility of that agency." Article 11, in its opinion, should grant discretionary authority to the Tribunal to withhold the reasons on which a judgment is based.[63]

On other matters the Committee held these views:

(i) *Article 2*: The competence of the Tribunal should be strictly limited to applications alleging non-observance of contracts or terms of appointment. The Secretary-General must be free to decide questions relating to the professional competence of a staff member, as well as questions relating to cases of serious misconduct and eventual disciplinary action to be taken on the basis of appropriate provisions of the staff regulations. The Tribunal must not become a negotiating body or an arbiter standing between the Secretary-General and the staff.

(ii) *Article 2*: It is important to preserve the concept that the staff regulations and rules to be interpreted by the Tribunal are those in force at the time of *alleged non-observance*.

(iii) *Article 10*: It is also important to preserve the right of the Secretary-General to state that, in a particular case, the rescinding of a decision or the effecting of a specific performance is impossible or inadvisable and to request the Tribunal to decide upon a payment of compensation, if any, for the injury sustained.[64]

Concerning the memorandum of the Staff Committee outlined above, the Advisory Committee pointed out that disciplinary cases involving alleged nonobservance of contract would be within the jurisdiction of the Tribunal. Any extension of the Tribunal's competence beyond this was, according to the Committee, bound to result in "unwarranted interference with the executive." It also opposed the retention of the Appeals Board in addition to the proposed Tribunal, because "such an arrangement would be administratively cumbersome and would create confusion in that it would easily lead to conflicts of competence." What is more, the delays which would inevitably flow from the double procedure "would not be in the best interests of the staff." [65]

In addition to the above, there were a few other communications of some interest regarding the proposed Tribunal. The President of the International Court of Justice, for example, asked, in a letter addressed to the Secretary-General, that the provision in the draft statute conferring competence on the Tribunal to adjudicate disputes involving the staff of the Registry of the Court be deleted. He based his request on the grounds that the Statute of the Court vested the Court with an exclusive authority to appoint, dismiss, and discipline staff members of the Registry and that, consequently, the latter "already have a complete jurisdictional guarantee, even wider than that which they would enjoy if the competence of the Administrative Tribunal were extended to their applications." [66]

The World Health Organization communicated to the Fifth Committee its views on the Tribunal's competence over disciplinary action. It expressed concern over the proposed exclusion from the Tribunal's competence of disputes arising out of disciplinary action. This, it feared, would make it difficult for the W.H.O. to make use of the Tribunal, because the health organization's staff regulations specifically provided for referral of such disputes to "a tribunal of an arbitral character which may be designated or, if necessary, established by the Executive Board until definitive arrangements have been made with the United Nations." Nor could the W.H.O. deprive its staff members of acquired contractual rights by amending its staff regulations to conform to the Tribunal's statute.[67]

The Fifth Committee thus had before it reports setting forth divergent points of view regarding various aspects of the proposal to establish an Administrative Tribunal. It was now in a position to weigh the merits of each argument and to attempt to map out a balanced blueprint for the Tribunal.

The Fifth Committee, in numerous meetings held during the period September 29, to November 8, 1949, gave lengthy and careful consideration to the above reports and recommendations.[68] Principal points raised by various delegations in the course of the general discussion were as follows:

1. Whether or not the Tribunal should be competent to hear and pass judgment upon applications with respect to disciplinary measures and to give advisory opinions at the request of the Secretary-General or of the Staff Committee;

2. Whether judgments should state the reasons on which they are based;

3. The relation of the Tribunal to the present Appeals Board under the Secretary-General's proposed revision of Staff Regulation 23;

4. The desirability of requiring that applicants deposit a sum of money at the time of filing an application with the Tribunal;

5. The payment of compensation in lieu of the rescinding of a contested decision of the Secretary-General;

6. The number and method of appointment of members of the Tribunal.[69]

Additionally, pro and con opinions were voiced on the desirability of setting up an Administrative Tribunal at that juncture in the Organization's administrative development. Certain delegations, expressing their doubts on this point, argued that since the Secretary-General needed wide discretionary powers equal to the responsibilities laid upon him by the Charter, the General Assembly should proceed cautiously and that the interests of the staff would be adequately protected in the meantime by retaining the existing machinery of the Appeals Board. On the other hand, many delegations felt that it would be in the interests of equity and of staff morale, as well as to the advantage of the administration, to have an independent judicial body such as the proposed tribunal for adjudication of disputes. They argued that the knowledge that such a means of redress was at the disposal of the staff would in itself remove many of the present causes of discontent and exercise a good influence on the relations between the administration and the staff.[70]

In the meantime both the Secretary-General and the delegations submitted further amendments to the draft statute. As a result, a number of prior amendments were withdrawn by those who had submitted them. These amendments concerned the authority of the General Assembly or of the Secretary-General acting on instructions of the General Assembly to alter at any time the rules and regulations of the Organization, the retention of the Appeals Board, the question of procedures and time limits for the filing of applications, the competence of the Tribunal to pass judgment on disciplinary cases and to give advisory opinions, and the requirement of a deposit of money in connection with the filing of application.[71]

Before we turn to the main decisions reached by the Fifth Committee, we may briefly survey the positions taken by some of the more active participants in the lengthy debate that took place in the meetings of the Committee. The countries which showed special interest in the debate included Australia, Belgium, Brazil, Canada, China, Colombia, Egypt, France, Great Britain, Haiti, Israel, Mexico, Norway, Pakistan, Poland, Union of South Africa, U.S.S.R., United States, Uruguay, and Venezuela. Of these, Belgium, Colombia, France, Norway, and Poland took the floor more than three times. In addition, a representative of the Legal Department of the Secretariat and the chairman of the Advisory Committee on Administrative and Budgetary Questions were on hand to answer questions.[72] Of the positions taken by various delegations, the following appear to merit attention:

1. The United States insisted that the General Assembly had the right to decide whether a member of the Tribunal was to be relieved of his duties. Australia and Pakistan supported this view. Belgium, however, pointed out that it was a well-recognized principle, at least in European countries, that the members of a tribunal could not be dismissed. Therefore, only the Tribunal itself should have the power to remove its members, it was argued. France and Norway shared this view.

2. The Union of South Africa objected to the provision empowering the President of the Tribunal to order the Secretary-General to suspend the execution of a decision. It was enough, in case of an unjustified injury to an official, that the official should receive compensation. This view was echoed by the U.S.S.R., which felt that to give the Tribunal such an authority would infringe Article

97 of the Charter which declared the Secretary-General to be the chief administrative officer of the United Nations. Belgium and Uruguay disagreed. They stressed that the proposed Tribunal would be a judicial organ which might have to rectify certain decisions of the Secretary-General, who was not infallible. Irreparable injury must therefore be prevented to the extent that it was feasible.

3. Colombia maintained that Article 10 established a tribunal which was in reality no tribunal—the proposed group was not really concerned with redressing injustice; it simply paid compensation. Colombia formally moved that the last sentence of Article 10, i.e., "but if such rescinding or specific performance is, in the opinion of the Secretary-General, impossible or inadvisable, the Tribunal shall order the payment to the applicant of compensation for injury sustained," be deleted. In support of the Colombian amendment Brazil said that Article 10 as it stood would fundamentally alter the intended nature of the Administrative Tribunal as it would give the Secretary-General the power to change a decision taken by the Tribunal. It was pointed out that although the Fifth Committee had the utmost confidence in the Secretary-General's judgment, in principle, no man could be considered infallible and that this was the very rationale behind the decision to establish an Administrative Tribunal. Moreover, not only did the proposal for monetary compensation represent a false concept of justice, but it would constitute an added financial burden on the United Nations. Haiti and Mexico expressed their support for this view.

On the other hand, Belgium pointed out that in cases where specific performance might be impossible, monetary compensation was indeed the only satisfactory course of action. Moreover, particularly from an administrative point of view, in the case of the United Nations, enforcement of specific performance might offer serious disadvantages in the functioning of the Secretariat. It was further explained that under Article 10 as it stood, the Secretary-General would not have any authority to revoke the Administrative Tribunal's decisions, but would merely make recommendations from the administrative point of view. Norway, Australia, France, and the United States joined in voicing their agreement with the Belgian position. Australia saw little room for abuse in Article

10 as it stood. Not only did the Administrative Tribunal itself provide a safeguard, but the Fifth Committee could also exercise surveillance over the Secretary-General's decision.

Poland took a middle-of-the-road position and suggested that Article 10 be redrafted in such a way as to give the Secretary-General a right of veto in exceptional cases where he could not comply with the decision reached by the Administrative Tribunal. The chairman of the Fifth Committee suggested, in this connection, that the words "but if such rescinding or specific performance is . . ." should be amended to read "but if, in exceptional cases, such rescinding or specific performance is . . . ." Colombia was agreeable to this latter proposal. China offered two alternative amendments, of which the second, namely, that the word "Secretary-General" should be replaced by the word "Tribunal," was accepted by Colombia, which then withdrew her own amendment. Mexico endorsed the same amendment. Uruguay, also in favor of the amendment, proposed changes in wording. The United States supported the Polish amendment on the ground that the Secretary-General was in the best position to decide the question. The Polish proposal was subsequently adopted by the Committee by 29 votes to 4, with 8 abstentions.

The main decisions of the Committee may now be catalogued:

1. Article 1 of the draft statute was approved. It is interesting to note that the U.S.S.R. delegation made an abortive attempt to change the title of the Tribunal to "Staff Claims Board" on the ground that the term "Administrative Tribunal" did not adequately or correctly reflect the character and competence of the proposed organ.

2. In accordance with the wish of the International Court of Justice, it was decided to delete reference in Article 2 to the Registry of the Court. It was further decided to strike out the provision relating to the competence of the Tribunal to give advisory opinion. Two points were emphasized in the course of the discussion regarding the Tribunal's competence: (a) that the Tribunal would not have jurisdiction in disciplinary cases unless such cases came within the terms of paragraph 1 of Article 2 and (b) that the Tribunal would have to respect the authority of the General Assembly to make such alterations and adjustments in the Staff Regulations as circumstances might require.

3. It was decided to reduce the number of Tribunal members

from seven to five. The recommendation of the Advisory Committee that the members should be appointed by the General Assembly was approved. In view of this decision the United States delegation withdrew its proposed addition to paragraph 1 of Article 3 which read: "In the choice of members of the Tribunal, administrative training and experience shall be recognized on a par with legal training and experience and judicial service." The amendment was withdrawn, however, on the condition that the text would be included in the Committee's report.

4. Another United States amendment to provide that dismissal of a member of the Tribunal could take place only on a two-thirds majority vote of the General Assembly was accepted. This, as noted, evoked strong objections from a number of delegations, which argued that according to a well-recognized principle such a decision should be exclusively within the power of the judicial organ concerned. They also feared that the amendment might have the effect of giving the Tribunal a political character.

5. It was further decided to delete the provision relating to the authority of the President of the Tribunal to order, in exceptional cases, suspension of a decision of the Secretary-General. The arguments which preceded this decision were already examined.

6. Article 10 of the draft statute authorizing the Tribunal to order the payment to the applicant of compensation for the injury sustained if, in the opinion of the Secretary-General, the rescinding of the decision contested or the specific performance of the obligation invoked was impossible or inadvisable was approved with minor revision. As already noted, however, this was the most controversial part of the draft statute. Many delegations were apprehensive that it would have a crippling effect on the authority and effectiveness of the Tribunal.

The draft statute as a whole, incorporating the amendments indicated above, was approved by the Committee on November 8, 1949, by 39 votes to 2, with 2 abstentions. The Committee also agreed unanimously to accept the consequential revision of Staff Regulation 23 as proposed by the Secretary-General.

At a later meeting of the Committee, additional amendments were proposed jointly by Belgium, Egypt, France, Netherlands, and Venezuela. These dealt with three points: the number of members of the Tribunal would be increased from five to seven; a member of the Tribunal would be dismissed by the General

Assembly only when the other members were of the unanimous opinion that he was unsuited for further service; and there would be two, rather than a single, Vice-Presidents. These amendments were subsequently adopted by the Committee.[73]

The remarks made by Mme. Bastid of the French delegation in introducing the amendments are worth noting. She said:

> This [the creation of an Administrative Tribunal] is in the interest of the staff members themselves, who will lose the impression, whether or not it is justified, that a more or less arbitrary power can be exercised against them and impair their moral and material situation. They will have the security given by a judge, a security which should be involved in any legal relations. . . . This international civil service will be reaffirmed and strengthened by the creation of this tribunal which will be entrusted with ensuring respect for the rules of the organizations. [Interpretation from French]

She added that employment conditions of staff members should be such as to permit the best functioning of the large United Nations administration, "an administration whose tasks and structure exceed in complexity everything that has existed up to the present time." The proposed Tribunal, she said, would be "the vigilant guardian of that legality." [74]

The draft statute submitted by the Fifth Committee, with amendments, was adopted intact by the General Assembly on November 24, 1949. The resolution establishing the Administrative Tribunal [resolution 351 (IV)] specified that the Statute would come into force on January 1, 1950. [75]

Upon the recommendation of the Fifth Committee, the General Assembly on December 9, 1949, adopted a resolution appointing the first members of the Tribunal. Appointed for a three-year term, to begin on January 1, 1950, were: Mme. Paul Bastid of France; Lt. General His Highness Maharaja Jam Shri Digvijay-asinhji Sahib of India; and Omar Loutfi of Egypt. The other members were: (for a two-year term) Rowland Egger of the United States and Emilio N. Oribe of Uruguay; (for a one-year term) Sir Sydney Caine of Great Britain and Vladimir Outrata of Czecho-slovakia.[76]

The Tribunal held its first plenary session at Lake Success from June 1, to 7, 1950. It elected a President and two Vice-Presidents, and adopted its rule of procedure. Of the seven members of the Tribunal six attended the plenary session, one member, namely,

Omar Loutfi, having tendered his resignation. The Tribunal then went into an ordinary session, attended by the President, two Vice-Presidents, and one alternate member. It undertook preliminary considerations of fifteen applications and one intervention. Upon the completion of the dossier, the Tribunal was formally seized of the cases on June 27, 1950. [77]

CHAPTER 3

THE
STRUCTURAL FRAMEWORK

THERE ARE TWO legal distinguishing marks of international administrative tribunals: international character and competence over
individuals. This was summed up by the International Court of
Justice in the following terms: "The Court does not deny that
the Administrative Tribunal [of the I.L.O.] is an international
tribunal. However, the question submitted to the Tribunal was
not a dispute between States. It was a controversy between Unesco
and one of its officials." [1]

There is little doubt that international administrative tribunals,
as the very name implies, are international in character. The disputes adjudicated by them are not those arising within the walls
of a particular state but those transcending national boundaries.
As we have already seen, theirs is a jurisdiction encompassing
disputes between an international organization on the one hand
and its employees on the other.[2]

What is more, international administrative tribunals have competence over individuals. Put another way, individuals enjoy access
to such tribunals. This sets the latter apart from the International
Court of Justice and its predecessor, the Permanent Court of International Justice. The International Court, as was the case with the
Permanent Court, is open only to States. Indeed this very fact
has provided an important *raison d'etre* of international administrative tribunals.

On what specific legal basis has the Tribunal been created? The
Charter, it may safely be asserted, provides a legal basis for the

Tribunal. Under paragraph 1 of Article 101, the General Assembly is empowered to establish regulations governing the personnel administration of the Organization. By virtue of Article 22, it is further authorized to "establish such subsidiary organs as it deems necessary for the performance of its functions."

Manifestly, these provisions clothe the General Assembly with full authority to create any organ, be it judicial or advisory, intended to deal with personnel disputes within the United Nations. This view was expressed by the International Court of Justice in its advisory opinion on the effect of the Tribunal's judgments.[3]

To say, however, that the creation of the Tribunal was consistent with the provisions of the Charter is but an incomplete explanation of its juridical basis. For the question remains, why are staff members subject to the jurisdiction of the Tribunal? The answer, according to Mme. Bastid, is to be found in the legal tie (*le lien juridique*) between them and the international organization. This tie is embodied in the staff members' contract, the terms of which are fixed unilaterally and with the administrative requirements of the Organization in view.[4]

The contract, however, is a voluntary agreement; parties to it sign it out of their own free will. By signing his contract, the staff member agrees to comply with duly established regulations of the Organization. As Mme. Bastid puts it: "Ainsi la base juridique de la compétence de la juridiction administrative internationale à l'égard des individus se trouve dans le contrat d'engagement, lorseque le statut du Tribunal est établi par une résolution interne de l'organisation."[5] In short, both the Charter and the contract entered into by staff members provide the legal basis of the Tribunal.

The Tribunal, by the explicit intent of its creators, was designed as an independent judicial organ. This fact was authoritatively reaffirmed by an advisory opinion of the International Court of Justice on July 13, 1954. The Court dwelt, *inter alia*, on whether the Tribunal was established either as a judicial body, or as an advisory organ, or a mere subordinate committee of the General Assembly.[6]

It examined several provisions of the Tribunal's Statute, such as:

Article 1: "A Tribunal is established by the present Statute to be known as the United Nations Administrative Tribunal."

Article 2:

paragraph 1: "The Tribunal shall be competent to hear and pass judgment upon applications . . ."

paragraph 3: "In the event of a dispute as to whether the Tribunal has competence, the matter shall be settled by the decision of the Tribunal."

Article 10:

paragraph 2: "The judgments shall be final and without appeal."

paragraph 3: "The judgments shall state the reasons on which they are based." [7]

It then declared:

These provisions and the terminology used are evidence of the judicial nature of the Tribunal. Such terms as "tribunal," "judgment," "competence to pass judgment upon applications," are generally used with respect to judicial bodies. The above–mentioned provisions of Articles 2 and 10 are of an essentially judicial character and conform with rules generally laid down in statutes or laws issued for courts of justice, such as, for instance, in the Statute of the International Court of Justice, Article 36, paragraph 6, Article 56, paragraph 1, Article 60, first sentence . . . .[8]

The Statute of the Tribunal, the Court went on, contains no provision attributing an advisory character to its functions. On the contrary, it ensures the independence of members of the Tribunal in Article 3, paragraph 1, by providing that "No member of the Tribunal can be dismissed by the General Assembly unless the other members are of the unanimous opinion that he is unsuited for further service." (Art. 3, par. 1) It further provides, the Court noted, that the Tribunal shall, if it finds that the application is well founded, order the rescinding of the decision contested or the specific performance of the obligation invoked.[9]

In the Court's opinion, the power to issue such orders to the chief administrative officer of the Organization could hardly have been conferred on an advisory organ or a subordinate committee. It thus concluded:

. . . the Tribunal is established, not as an advisory organ or a mere subordinate committee of the General Assembly, but as an independent and truly judicial body pronouncing final judgments without appeal within the limited field of its functions.[10]

To sum up, the Tribunal is an international court competent to settle disputes between individuals, i.e., staff members on one side and the Organization on the other. Its legal basis lies both in the Charter and in the staff member's employment contract. Furthermore, it is a truly judicial organ, and not an advisory body nor a mere adjunct to the General Assembly.

The organization of the Tribunal is marked by its simplicity, for which the original framers of the Statute deserve credit. The Advisory Committee on a Statute for a United Nations Administrative Tribunal, to which reference was made earlier, took particular pains to ensure "a simple organization and an expeditious procedure." The present Statute bears an unmistakable imprint of the Committee's effort. We shall deal with the procedure for appointing members, their compensation as well as legal status, the duties of the President and Vice-Presidents, the composition and work of the Tribunal's secretariat, and the Tribunal's finances.

The first two paragraphs of Article 3 of the Statute now in force stipulate the following with regard to appointment of members:

1. The Tribunal shall be composed of seven members, no two of whom may be nationals of the same State. Only three shall sit in any particular case.

2. The members shall be appointed by the General Assembly for three years, and they may be re-appointed; provided, however, that of the members initially appointed, the terms of two members shall expire at the end of one year and the terms of two members shall expire at the end of two years. A member appointed to replace a member whose term of office has not expired shall hold office for the remainder of his predecessor's term.[11]

In accordance with these provisions, the General Assembly annually appoints two or three members of the Tribunal.

Since an almost identical procedure is followed every year, it will suffice to describe the procedure followed in recent appointments. At the seventeenth session of the General Assembly Secretary-General U Thant initiated the process of filling vacancies in the Tribunal by sending a note to the General Assembly. In the note, he first cited the relevant provisions of the Statute and included the roster of the Tribunal's present membership. He then noted that three vacancies would occur due to the expiration of the terms of office of two members and to the resignation of one member. Recalling that at previous sessions the Fifth Committee, after a secret ballot, had submitted to the General Assembly a draft resolution containing the names of the persons recommended for appointment to the Tribunal, the Secretary-General suggested a similar procedure should be followed.[12]

The item was included in the agenda recommended by the General Committee on September 21, 1962. The agenda was subsequently adopted by the General Assembly. The Fifth Committee took up the question on November 28, 1962. It had before it names of four candidates—two for vacancies due to occur on December 31, 1962. [13] The curricula vitae of the candidates had been previously furnished by the Secretariat.[14]

The Committee by a secret ballot decided on the names of candidates to be recommended for appointment. The draft resolution adopted by the Committee and recommended to the General Assembly read:

The General Assembly

1. *Appoints* the following persons as members of the United Nations Administrative Tribunal:

> Mr. James W. Barco,
> The Right Honourable Lord Crook,
> Mr. Louis Ignacio-Pinto;

2. *Declares* Mr. Barco and Lord Crook to be appointed for a three-year term beginning on 1 January 1963, and Mr. Ignacio-Pinto to be appointed for a period beginning on the date of the present resolution and ending on 31 December 1964. [15]

The above recommendation was carried out in full on December 11, 1962, when the General Assembly adopted an identically-worded resolution.[16]

Until 1960 members of the Tribunal were paid only travel and subsistence allowances for attending sessions at a uniform rate set by the General Assembly for members of organs and subsidiary organs of the United Nations. The Secretary-General, however, had made an abortive attempt to provide for the payment of an honorarium. In the budget estimates for the financial year 1959, Hammarskjöld provided for the payment of an honorarium to the President and other members of the Tribunal "in recognition of the importance of the functions of the Tribunal and of the time its members are compelled to devote to matters before it, both during and between its sessions." [17]

The provision was deleted by the General Assembly, which acted on the recommendation of the Advisory Committee on Administrative and Budgetary Questions. The latter had suggested the deletion on the ground that a decision of principle was involved. In the budget estimates for the financial year 1961 the Secretary-General again took up the question. He pointed out that members of the Tribunal devoted a considerable amount of time to the study of cases on the list before each session. This resulted generally in short sessions, thus reducing the expenses borne by the Organization. Furthermore, he said, the President of the Tribunal had an additional burden—"time-consuming administrative duties." [18]

For these reasons, Hammarskjöld continued to believe that "the payment of an honorarium would be appropriate so as to recognize in a token manner the time and effort devoted to the work of the Tribunal." He therefore proposed that an annual honorarium of $500 be paid to the president of the Tribunal and that, in addition, an honorarium of $250 each be paid to the president and the other members of the Tribunal for each session of the Tribunal attended by them. He estimated that, if approved, his proposals would require an additional provision of $2,500 for 1961 and future years.[19]

In an annex attached to the proposals the Secretary-General underlined the fact that in accordance with a 1957 decision of the General Assembly, the chairman of the Advisory Committee on Administrative and Budgetary Questions; the president and other members of the Permanent Central Opium Board; the president and other members of the Drug Supervisory Body; and the chairman, special rapporteurs, and other members of the International Law Commission were already being paid honoraria ranging from $300 to $5,000. [20]

The Advisory Committee on Administrative and Budgetary Questions, after reexamining the question, decided to support the Secretary-General's proposals. In reaching its decision, the Committee recalled that the Tribunal was the only one among the three specific organs considered in 1954 to which the payment of honoraria was denied. It further noted that "the average volume of documentation submitted to the Tribunal, mostly for preparatory study, has amounted to some 280 pages per case." It also wished to stress the importance of admitting no further exceptions to the basic rule of not making any payments to include an element of fee or remuneration.[21]

On the basis of these documents, the Fifth Committee considered the question on October 11 and 14, 1960. The positions taken by various delegations during the Committee's discussions included the following:

1. Appointment to expert bodies of the United Nations such

as the Administrative Tribunal conferred distinction on the individual as well as honor of his country, and it was not fitting that any payment, other than for subsistence and travel expenses, should be made in respect of services rendered.

2. Since the General Assembly had already departed from the principle of not authorizing the payment of honoraria, the withholding of honoraria from members of the Tribunal appeared discriminatory.

3. The whole question of the payment of honoraria should be reviewed in relation to the position of principle originally taken by the General Assembly. In the meantime, some delegations favored the payment of honoraria to members of the Tribunal on a provisional basis. Others opposed any such payment pending the outcome of the review.[22]

Meanwhile, a representative of the Secretary-General stressed that for the proper consideration of cases the members were often called upon to study, in advance of a session, voluminous submissions, at times running to several hundred pages. It was also pointed out that there was no valid reason for drawing a distinction between the Tribunal, on the one hand, and the International Law Commission, the Permanent Central Opium Board, and the Drug Supervisory Body, on the other. The Secretary-General's proposals therefore were based on the principle of uniformity of treatment of the members of expert bodies. The Committee finally approved the proposals, incorporating the recommendations of the Advisory Committee which wanted to make it clear that honoraria would apply only to the sessions devoted to the considerations of cases.[23]

The legal position of members of the Tribunal vis-à-vis the Organization may be described as that of an "agent." The International Court of Justice has interpreted this to mean "any person who, whether a paid official or not, and whether permanently employed or not, has been charged by an organ of the organization with carrying out, or helping to carry out, one of its functions— in short, any person through whom it acts." [24]

From the above it follows that the provisions of the General Convention on the Privileges and Immunities of the United Nations regarding experts in mission (Art. VI) apply to members of the Tribunal.[25] As members of a judicial organ, they must necessarily enjoy a large measure of independence. Accordingly, they are given a special legal guarantee against dismissal in the Statute:

only when all the other members are of the unanimous opinion that he is unsuited for further service can a member of the Tribunal be dismissed.[26]

Membership in the Tribunal is not incompatible with service as a governmental representative on legislative committees of the General Assembly.[27] Nor is it a bar to holding a remunerative position or practicing professions outside the Organization. In short, being a member of the Tribunal is not a full-time job; it only requires a part–time service. The members are otherwise engaged in their respective professional or public service activities.

No provision is to be found in the Statute regarding the desired qualifications of members of the Tribunal. In practice, the majority of members have had legal training and experience. Several members have been persons with experience in handling employer-employee disputes. Mme. Bastid feels, however, that experience with employment disputes has no relevance for the tasks of the Tribunal, not only because the Tribunal applies laws, and not the rules of equity, but also because it follows a judicial procedure which is different from the techniques often utilized in the adjustment of industrial disputes.[28]

The Statute does provide, however, that each of the seven members must be a national of different states.[29] This, to some extent, ensures an equitable geographical representation. It does not, however, necessarily guarantee the representation of diverse systems of law, which Mme. Bastid believes is essential "pour assurer l'autorité de jugements et donner pratiquement une base suffisamment large à l'utilisation—qui demeure inévitable—des principes genéraux du droit." [30]

In the 14–year period from 1950 to 1963 a total of twenty two persons have served as members of the Tribunal. Of these five have served more than three terms. Mme. Bastid, currently President of the Tribunal at the time of this study, has held her membership in the Tribunal during the entire period. It is interesting to note (see Table 1) that only twelve states have thus far been represented [31] in the Tribunal's membership, namely, Czechoslovakia, Dahomey, Ecuador, Egypt, France, India, Iran, Sweden, the United Kingdom, the United States, Uruguay, and Venezuela. Five Americans, three Uruguayans, and two each from Ecuador, Egypt, India, and the United Kingdom have been members of the Tribunal. With the exception of 1952 and 1953, during which no

U. S. national served on the Tribunal, France, the United Kingdom, and the United States have always been represented.

The Tribunal elects, at its annual plenary session, a President, a first Vice-President, and a second Vice-President. They serve for one year and may be reelected. Should the President or a Vice-President cease to be a member of the Tribunal before the expiration of his normal term, an election is held to appoint a successor. The election, in case of a vacancy of a Vice-President, may be conducted by correspondence.[32]

Table 1

THE ROSTER OF THE MEMBERSHIP OF THE UNITED NATIONS
ADMINISTRATIVE TRIBUNAL, 1950-1963[a]

Members	Year					
	1950	1951	1952	1953	1954	1955
Mme. Paul Bastid (France)	x	x	x	x	x	x
Sir Sydney Caine (UK)	x					
Lt. Gen. Digvijayasinhji (India)[b]	x	x	x			
Rowland Andrews Egger (USA)	x	x				
Omar Loutfi (Egypt)	res.[c]			x	x	x
Emilio N. Oribe (Uruguay)	x	x				
Vladimir Outrata (Czechoslovakia)	x	x	x	x		
Hamed Sultan (Egypt)	x	x	x			
The Right Honourable Lord Crook (UK)		x	x	x	x	x
Homero Viteri Lafronte (Ecuador)			x	x	x	
Bror Arvid Sture Petrén (Sweden)			x	x	x	x
Djalal Abdoh (Iran)				x	x	x
Jacob Mark Lashly (USA)					x	x
V. M. Pérez-Perozo (Venezuela)						x
R. Venkataraman (India)						
Francisco A. Forteza (Uruguay)						
Harold Riegelman (USA)						
James J. Casey (USA)						
José A. Correa (Ecuador)						
Héctor Gros Espiell (Uruguay)						
James W. Barco (USA)						
Louis Ignacio-Pinto (Dahomey)						

Table 1—*Continued*

Members	Year							
	1956	1957	1958	1959	1960	1961	1962	1963
Bastid	x	x	x	x	x	x	x	x
Caine								
Digvijayasinhji								
Egger								
Loutfi	x	x	x	x	x	x	res.	
Oribe								
Outrata								
Sultan								
Crook	x	x	x	x	x	x	x	x
Lafronte								
Petrén	x	x	x	x	x	x	x	x
Abdoh								
Lashly	x	x	res.					
Pérez-Perozo	x							
Venkataraman	x	x	x	x	x	x	x	x
Forteza		x	x	x	x			
Riegelman				x				
Casey					x	x	x	
Correa						res.		
Espiell						x	x	x
Barco								x
Ignacio-Pinto								x

aCompiled from resolutions adopted by the General Assembly, 1949-1962, inclusive.

bThe full name and title read: Lt. General His Highness Maharja Jam Shri Digvijayasinhji Sahib.

cResigned.

The President is entrusted with three principal tasks: directing the work of the Tribunal and of its secretariat; representing the Tribunal in all administrative matters; and presiding at the meetings of the Tribunal. If he is unable to act, he can designate one of the Vice-Presidents to act in his place. In the absence of any such designation by the President, the first Vice-President or, in the event of the latter's incapacity, the second Vice-President acts as President. No case can be heard by the Tribunal except under the chairmanship of the President or one of the Vice-Presidents.[33]

Under the Statute the Secretary-General is obligated to "provide the Tribunal with an Executive Secretary and such other staff as may be considered necessary." [34] It is further stipulated that the Secretary-General "shall make the administrative arrangements necessary for the functioning of the Tribunal." [35] These provisions constitute the legal basis of the Tribunal's secretariat, which plays a vitally important role in the operation of the Tribunal.

In fact, it may be said that the secretariat,[36] functioning on a year-round basis, physically symbolizes the continued existence of the Tribunal which meets only sporadically. However, its chief function clearly is more than symbolic; it performs the administrative and clerical tasks which are indispensable to the functioning of the Tribunal. Aside from the usual administrative duties, it also compiles and publishes the judgments of the Tribunal.

Located on the thirty-fourth floor of the Secretariat Building of the United Nations in New York City, the secretariat is currently staffed by an Executive Secretary and a secretary. The Executive Secretary, Nicholas Teslenko, *Docteur en Droit* (Paris), of France, concurrently serves as a senior officer in the Office of Legal Affairs. Similarly, his secretary, Mrs. Doriane Kurz, an American, is a correspondence officer of the same office. When the Tribunal is in session, such additional personnel as verbatim reporters and interpreters are loaned to the secretariat from the Department of Conference and General Services. Additional clerical help is also made available.[37]

While the secretariat is thus closely tied to the Secretariat of the United Nations, physically and in other ways, it nevertheless enjoys a large measure of operational autonomy and independence. As the incumbent Executive Secretary puts it, "as far as the Tribunal is concerned, nobody can give me any orders" except the President of the Tribunal. As an illustration of the complete independence of the Tribunal's secretariat, he points out that although the United Nations has a system of centralized files, the Tribunal keeps its own files. Additionally, the secretariat is not subject to the U.N.'s centralized postal inspection whereby all outgoing mail is checked; the Executive Secretary has full control over the Tribunal's mail.[38]

The expenses of the Tribunal are borne by the United Nations.[39] The Tribunal has no budget of its own, nor does it appear as a separate item in the budget of the United Nations, as is the case with the International Court of Justice. The differential treatment is, perhaps, explainable in terms of the legal status of the two bodies —the World Court is a principal judicial organ of the United Nations, the Tribunal is but a subsidiary judicial organ. Moreover, the size and jurisdictional scope of the two are by no means comparable.

CHAPTER 4

OPERATIVE MECHANISMS

THE BASIC ATTRIBUTES of man-made institutions, like the human body, are both static and dynamic. Hence, the dichotomized approach to the study of the human body—anatomy and physiology—can be conveniently duplicated in an inquiry into institutions created by human fiat. In other words, such institutions can and must be described in terms not only of their structural idiosyncrasies but also of their functional characteristics.

The first task has already been assayed in the foregoing two chapters, where we have explored the historical background as well as the organizational framework of the Tribunal. In this chapter we tackle the latter task: description of the *modus operandi* of the Tribunal. Topics of relevance are the competence, procedure, and practice of the Tribunal; the law applicable by it; the nature and effect of remedies available from it; and, finally, the review procedure for its judgments.

A preliminary question with regard to the competence of the Tribunal is one of definition: What is the meaning of the term "competence" in legal parlance? This, however, begs another question: What, if any, is the distinction between the terms "competence" and "jurisdiction"? We shall start by exploring this latter question.

To give a straightforward answer, there is no precise legal distinction between the two terms. They are used interchangeably, not merely by international lawyers, but in the U.N. Charter and the Statute of the International Court of Justice as well. In so far as the World Court is concerned, however, Shabtai Rosenne notes that a distinction can be made between the two. He writes:

> . . . the Statute . . . limits the use of the word "jurisdiction" to contentious cases, and furthermore "jurisdiction" is the word mostly used by the Court in that connexion. On the other hand, the word "competence" is more frequently found in advisory opinions, sometimes being replaced by "power." In this context, it is suggested that, in so far as concerns the Court, "jurisdiction" is a stricter concept than "competence." Jurisdiction relates to the capacity of the Court to decide a concrete case with binding force. "Competence," on the other hand, is more subjective, including both jurisdiction and the element of the propriety of the Court's exercising its jurisdiction.[1]

Whatever merit Rosenne's argument may possess, it is clear that such a distinction cannot be applied to the Tribunal. For the Statute of the Tribunal is quite explicit as to the interchangeability of the two terms. Thus in Article 11, paragraph 1, we find an expression, "on the ground that the Tribunal has exceeded its jurisdiction *or* competence . . ." [Italics mine]. If we examine the Statute as a whole, however, we find that the term "competence" is given a patently preferential treatment.[2] This is in contrast to the Statute of the Court where "jurisdiction" is used more frequently.[3]

In short, we may be justified in asserting that the terms "competence" and "jurisdiction" can be used interchangeably but that the former is more appropriate for our purposes in view of its more frequent appearance in the Statute of the Tribunal.

Competence or jurisdiction, as a *terminus technicus*, refers to the power of a judicial body to "do justice" between the litigating parties, i.e., "to decide the question before it with binding force."[4] The expression "do justice," Rosenne points out, has been used by the Court several times. For instance, the Court noted, in its advisory opinion concerning the competence of the Tribunal, that the Tribunal was set up "to do justice between the Organization and the staff members."[5] It also enumerated the functions of a judicial organ, namely, "considering the arguments of the parties, appraising the evidence produced by them, establishing the facts and declaring the law applicable to them."[6]

Broadly speaking, the competence of international tribunals may be divided into two categories—"competence with respect to persons" and "competence with respect to subject-matter." [7] The former is referred to as competence *ratione personae,* and the latter as competence *ratione materiae.*[8] In addition, competence *ratione temporis* is sometimes discussed. This concerns the temporal dimension of competence, i.e., from what point in time does the competence of a tribunal commence?

To reiterate, we do not make any distinction between the terms "competence" and "jurisdiction" but use them interchangeably. The expression competence *or* jurisdiction, then, refers to the power of a tribunal to do justice—to decide the question before it with binding force. It involves three aspects, persons, subject matter, and time.

Competence Ratione Personae

Access to the Tribunal is granted to two main categories of persons—any staff member of the U.N. Secretariat even after his employment has ceased and his successor(s) *mortis causa,* and any other person who can establish that he is entitled to rights under any contract or terms of appointment, including the provisions of staff regulations and rules upon which the staff member could have relied.[9]

There are certain categories of persons who do not normally come under the definition of staff members of the Secretariat and who, unless otherwise entitled to contractual rights as indicated above, are excluded from the jurisdiction of the Tribunal. One criterion of a staff member of the Secretariat is whether or not his legal status is regulated by the Staff Regulations and Rules. Among those who do not meet this criterion are the Secretary-General, those who have been locally recruited for manual or technical work, and those who serve the Organization only briefly.[10]

The authority, responsibility, and conditions of service of the Secretary-General are set forth in the Charter; hence he is not included in the category of staff members, whom he appoints by virtue of the authority delegated to him by the General Assembly.[11] Furthermore, as the chief administrative officer of the Organization, the Secretary-General is called upon to represent the interest of the United Nations in disputes that are brought before the Tribunal by the persons to whom the Tribunal is open. In most disputes he is a respondent acting on behalf of the Organization which is a juridical person as recognized by the International Court of Justice.[12]

Thus, while the Secretary-General is almost invariably a legal representative of a party to disputes before the Tribunal, which, *stricto sensu*, is the United Nations itself, he does not, in his private capacity, enjoy access to the Tribunal in the sense that he may bring litigations against the Organization alleging nonobservance of his contractual rights.[13]

Those who have been locally recruited for manual or technical work are excluded from the benefit of the Staff Regulations and Rules. Their conditions of service are instead regulated by pertinent local laws and regulations governing employment relationship. This is logical in view of the fact that they cannot be regarded as international civil servants in the usual sense of the term.[14] The experts who serve on brief assignments of the Organization likewise normally stand outside the jurisdiction of the Staff Regulations and Rules. However, the Staff Rules have formally recognized the right of access to the Tribunal of those who are engaged in the Expanded Program of Technical Assistance.[15]

A delicate problem of application arises with respect to a successor *mortis causa*, or, in the phraseology of the Statute, "any person who has succeeded to the staff member's rights on his death." [16] Briefly stated, the problem is: how do you determine a "successor *mortis causa*"? In effect, this is a problem in private international law or conflict of laws. Normally, the national law of the country of which the deceased staff member was a national is applied. Another problem may arise in this connection, if there is more than one successor. This again has to be resolved in accordance with conflict of laws.[17]

In addition to the two categories of persons described above, there is another group of persons to whom the Tribunal is open on a limited basis. This group comprises staff members of the specialized agencies with which the Secretary-General has concluded special agreements in accordance with Article 14 of the Statute. To be more specific, the Tribunal is competent to hear and pass judgment upon application alleging nonobservance of the Regulations of the U.N. Joint Staff Pension Fund presented by (1) any staff member of a specialized agency which has made a special agreement mentioned above, even after his employment has ceased and his successor *mortis causa*; (2) any other person who can show that he is entitled to rights under the Regulations of the Pension Fund by virtue of the participation in the Fund of a staff member of a specialized agency described above.[18]

In the special agreement, the specialized agency concerned agrees, *inter alia*, to accept the judgments of the Tribunal as final and without appeal and to give full effect to them. The Secretary-General, meanwhile, undertakes to make, in consultation with the agency concerned, the administrative arrangements necessary for the functioning of the Tribunal with respect to cases arising under such an agreement. The additional expenses which may be incurred by the United Nations in connection with the handling of cases arising under such an agreement are borne by the Pension Fund.[19] The Tribunal explicitly recognized the right of access enjoyed by persons in this category[20] and has entertained five applications involving them.[21]

Competence Ratione Materiae

The subject matter with which the Tribunal is competent to deal is alleged "nonobservance of contracts of employment of staff members of the Secretariat of the United Nations or of the terms of appointment of such staff members." The words "contracts" and "terms of appointment" include all pertinent regulations and rules in force at the time of alleged nonobservance, including the staff pension regulations.[22]

Specifically excluded from the competence *ratione materiae* of the Tribunal are disputes involving disciplinary measures taken against staff members and matters relating to the internal administration of the Organization. It will be recalled that the architects of the Tribunal repeatedly emphasized that the Tribunal would not interfere in matters relating to the conduct of administration, which they regarded as lying within the discretionary domain of the Secretary-General. That intention has been consistently honored in the judgments of the Tribunal.

The Tribunal is thus concerned solely with seeing that the employment rights of staff members as set forth in their contracts and other documents are fully respected; this means, in practice, that most disputes which come before it relate to the termination of appointment of staff members.

Competence Ratione Temporis

The Statute restricts the competence *ratione temporis* of the Tribunal to disputes which have arisen after January 1, 1950. Insofar as concerns applications where the cause of complaint arose prior to that date, the Tribunal is incompetent.[23] In conformity with a generally recognized rule governing the competence of international judicial tribunals,[24] the Tribunal reserves the power, in the event of a dispute as to whether it has competence, to decide its own competence.[25] Thus in Judgment No. 28, the Tribunal had to decide whether it had competence to make final judgment and found that it lacked such competence.[26] In another case the competence of the Tribunal to hear the case was challenged by the Secretary-General on the grounds that the application was not receivable because it had been filed too late and that the applicant was not a member of the staff of the United Nations Secretariat and therefore was not entitled to resort to the Tribunal. The Tribunal, however, ruled that it had competence to hear the case.[27] A challenge of competence was also rejected in Judgment No. 70. [28]

The Tribunal is further competent to award costs to one of the parties. This competence, however, met with vigorous challenge by the Administration at the outset. The Legal Department (now the Office of Legal Affairs), in a memorandum to the Tribunal dated December 13, 1950, argued (1) that the Tribunal was without authority under its Statute to tax costs against the losing party and (2) that even if the Tribunal decided that it had competence to assess costs, as opposed to damages, they should be strictly limited and not include all types of "actual costs" as was permitted by the Tribunal in Judgment No. 2. [29] The Tribunal did not agree with the above view but reaffirmed in a later judgment its competence to award costs other than compensation for damages.[30]

While the Statute is silent on the Tribunal's competence to interpret its judgments, the Tribunal has in fact recognized and exercised such a competence. It declared:

The Tribunal finds that the competence of national and international courts to interpret their own judgments is generally recognized. It notes that article 6 of the Rules empowers the President of the Tribunal to designate the members sitting in each case and that article 19 permits the Tribunal to vary any time-limit fixed by the Rules.

The Tribunal therefore holds itself competent to consider the Motion requesting an interpretation of the judgments referred to above and declares that so far as the formal requirements are concerned, the Motion is receivable.[31]

In interpreting judgments, the Tribunal is guided by what it calls "the general principles regarding the interpretation of judgments" laid down by the International Court of Justice in the Asylum case (interpretation). The principles as quoted by the Tribunal are as follows:

(1) The real purpose of the request must be to obtain an interpretation of the judgment. This signifies that its object must be solely to obtain clarification of the meaning and the scope of what the Court has decided with binding force, and not to obtain an answer to questions not so decided. Any other construction of Article 60 of the Statute would nullify the provision of the article that the judgment is final and without appeal.

(2) In addition, it is necessary that there should exist a dispute as to the meaning or scope of the judgment.

To decide whether the first requirement stated above is fulfilled, one must bear in mind the principle that it is the duty of the Court not only to reply to the questions as stated in the final submissions of the parties, but also to abstain from deciding points not included in those submissions.

Interpretation can in no way go beyond the limits of the judgment fixed in advance by the Parties themselves in their submissions.[32]

In short, the Tribunal is competent to adjudicate upon disputes arising between staff members of the United Nations or their successors in interest on the one hand and the Organization on the other. However, the subject matter about which it can pronounce binding judgment is limited to alleged nonobservance of the staff members' contracts or of other pertinent regulations and rules. It further has competence, customarily enjoyed by international tribunals, to settle any dispute as to its own competence. In addition, it is competent to award legal costs and to interpret its own judgments.

The Tribunal does not function haphazardly or extemporaneously, but operates according to a prescribed procedure. The procedure is spelled out in the Statute and the Rules. When compared to the practice of municipal courts, however, the procedure followed in the Tribunal, or that followed in any international tribunal for that matter, is markedly flexible and informal.[33] The proceedings before the Tribunal are both written and oral. However, there are certain requirements which have to be fulfilled before proceedings can be formally instituted.

We have already seen that the recourse to the Tribunal is not the only remedy available to an aggrieved staff member. Also open to him is an administrative remedy, i.e., a recourse to the Joint Appeals Board. The Statute expressly provides that the staff member cannot avail himself of the legal protection afforded by the Tribunal unless he has first exhausted such an administrative remedy. The exception to this general rule is the case where the Secretary-General and the applicant have agreed to submit the application directly to the Tribunal.[34]

The staff member thus must first submit a dispute to the Joint Appeals Board and then wait for the Board to communicate its opinion to the Secretary-General. In the event that the Board's recommendations are favorable to the applicant, he can bring the case before the Tribunal only if the Secretary-General has (1) rejected the recommendations; (2) failed to take any action within the thirty days following the communication of the opinion; or (3) failed to carry out the recommendations within the thirty days following the communication of the opinion.[35]

If, on the other hand, the recommendations made by the Board and accepted by the Secretary-General are unfavorable to the applicant, then he can submit the dispute to the Tribunal provided the Board does not unanimously consider that it is frivolous.[36] In either case, the applicant must observe a time limit of ninety days, reckoned from the date either of the Secretary-General's action or inaction described above or of the communication of the Board's opinion containing recommendations unfavorable to him.[37]

If the Tribunal has not, at the time when an application becomes receivable, made public the date of its first session, the time limit of ninety days begins to run from the date of such an announcement. The time limit may also be extended to one year if the heirs of a deceased staff member or the trustee of a staff member who is not in a position to manage his own affairs, file the application in the name of the staff member. The Tribunal is further free to waive the time limit in any particular case. The filing of an application does not have the effect of suspending the execution of the decision contested.[38]

Applications instituting proceedings are submitted to the Tribunal through the Executive Secretary. They may be in any one of the five official languages of the United Nations. They must be divided into four sections: (1) information concerning the personal and official status of the applicant; (2) pleas; (3) explanatory statement; and (4) annexes. The first section, namely information concerning the personal and official status of the applicant, must be drawn in accordance with a form prescribed by the Tribunal and annexed to the Rules.[39]

The pleas must indicate all the measures and decisions which the applicant requests the Tribunal to order or take. They must spell out:

(a) Any preliminary or provisional measures, such as the production of additional documents or the hearing of witnesses, which the applicant is requesting the Tribunal to order before proceeding to consider the merits;

(b) The decisions which the applicant is contesting and whose rescission he is requesting under article 9, paragraph 1, of the Statute;

(c) The obligations which the applicant is invoking and whose specific performance he is requesting under article 9, paragraph 1, of the Statute;

(d) The amount of compensation claimed by the applicant in the event that the Secretary-General decides, in the interest of the United Nations, to pay compensation for the injury sustained in accordance with option given to him under article 9, paragraph 1, of the Statute;

(e) And any other relief which the applicant may request in accordance with the Statute.[40]

In the explanatory statement are set forth the facts and the legal grounds on which the pleas are based. The specific provisions of the contract of employment or of the terms of appointment whose nonobservance is alleged must therefore be included. Finally, the annexes contain the text of all documents referred to in the application.[41]

The applicant must prepare seven copies of the application, each of which must contain a statement certifying that it is a true copy of the original application. Both the original and seven copies of the application must bear the signature either of the applicant or of his legal representative in the event of the applicant's incapacity. The application must be filed within the time limit noted above. The 90–day limit also applies to the case where the Secretary-General and the applicant have agreed to submit the application directly to the Tribunal. The filing in such a case takes place within ninety days of the date on which the Secretary-General notifies the applicant of his agreement to direct submission.[42]

The time limit is extended to one year for both a successor

mortis causa to the staff member's rights and the legal representative of a staff member who is not in a position to manage his own affairs. The Executive Secretary of the Tribunal is charged with the task of seeing that the formal requirements described above are fulfilled. He may either call upon the applicant to make such corrections as he deems necessary in the application and the copies thereof or make the necessary corrections himself, provided the President of the Tribunal approves such a procedure. The latter course of action is taken when the defects in the application do not affect the substance.[43] The filing of an application does not have the effect of suspending the execution of the decision contested.[44] A few applicants, however, have made special requests for suspension of the Secretary-General's decisions. In those instances the Tribunal has considered "the general circumstances of the case" as well as the relevant legal provisions. No interim measure, however, has yet been ordered.[45]

After ascertaining that the formal requirements prescribed in the Rules are complied with, the Executive Secretary transmits a copy of the application to the respondent. Within thirty days of such transmission, the respondent must submit to the Tribunal through the Executive Secretary a duly signed original and seven copies of an answer. The answer, which may be written in any one of the working languages of the General Assembly, i.e., English and French, must include pleas, an explanatory statement, and annexes. A copy of the respondent's answer, when the latter's formal validity is ascertained, is then sent to the applicant.[46]

Within thirty days of the receipt of the respondent's answer, the applicant may file with the Executive Secretary written observations on it. The written observations must meet substantially the same requirements as those for the application. A copy of the observations is again transmitted to the respondent by the Executive Secretary.[47]

The President of the Tribunal may, either *proprio motu* or at the request of either party, call upon the parties to submit additional written statements or documents. These must be furnished in the original and seven properly authenticated copies each. Any document not drawn up in any of the five official languages of the United Nations must be accompanied by a certified translation into one of the working languages of the General Assembly. In order to complete the documentation of the case, the President may obtain any necessary information from any party, witnesses, or experts. He may designate a member of the Tribunal or any other disinterested person to take oral statements.[48]

When, in the opinion of the President, the documentation of a case is sufficiently complete, he instructs the Executive Secretary to place the case on the list. The Executive Secretary thereupon informs the parties of the inclusion of the case in the list.[49] It is at this stage that the Tribunal may be said to have been formally seized of the case. This is technically known as "seisin." [50] As soon as the date of opening of the session at which a case has been entered for hearing has been fixed, the Executive Secretary notifies the parties.[51]

The Executive Secretary is responsible for transmitting all documents and making all notifications required in connection with proceedings before the Tribunal. He is further charged with making for each case a dossier which records all actions taken in connection with the preparation of the case for trial, the dates thereof, and the dates on which any document or notification forming part of the procedure is received in or dispatched from his office.[52]

An applicant may either present his case before the Tribunal in person or designate a staff member of the United Nations or one of the specialized agencies to represent him. He may also be represented by counsel authorized to practice in any country a member of the organization concerned.[53] In order to facilitate such representation, the Secretary-General has made special administrative arrangements to maintain a panel of qualified staff members who will serve as counsel in cases before the Tribunal, the Appeals Board or the Disciplinary Committee. The members of the panel are appointed by the Secretary-General for a period of one year on the advice of the Staff Council and with their own consent. The names and qualifications of these persons are communicated to the staff from time to time by means of information circulars.[54]

Any applicant to the Tribunal is free either to designate his counsel from outside or to request counsel from the panel within the Secretariat. If the counsel who is so requested agrees to act in the case, then he is authorized and directed by the Secretary-General to assist in the preparation and presentation of the case as part of his official duties. This means, in effect, that the applicant is receiving free legal assistance at the expense of the Organization. What is more, the United Nations endeavors to obtain the visa and pays the necessary travel expenses if any travel is involved.[55] The panel of counsel for 1963 included the names of twenty-nine staff members together with brief notes on their education and experience.[56]

The flexibility of the procedure in the Tribunal may be seen in the fact that the above requirements may sometimes be waived by the President, if a party claims that he is unable to comply with them and if the waiver does not affect the substance of the application.[57] The above procedure has evolved out of more than a decade of trial and error. In December, 1952, three years after it began to function, the Tribunal was confronted with the problem of an unnecessarily prolonged procedure. In its annual note to the President of the General Assembly, the Tribunal commented:

> This [the prolonged procedure] has had at least two unfortunate results: In the most recent case (December 1952), the hearing of the case commenced on the anniversary of the day on which the Applicant left the employment of the United Nations in the preceding year. In the event of a judgment in favour of the Applicant, therefore, one complete year's pay would be involved as an automatic payment.
>
> In an earlier case, in August 1952, there was the other result that the Tribunal was considering a case in the light of Staff Regulations operative in 1951, whereas in February 1952, the General Assembly had adopted new Staff Regulations and had given the Secretary-General new powers. No decision of the Tribunal can completely obviate that position, but if the cases can be heard by the Tribunal within a more reasonable period of time, there will be less risk of a decision of the Tribunal causing confusion in the minds of the Secretariat as to the Regulations and Rules in force.[58]

The Rules of the Tribunal have since been amended four times— in 1954, 1955, 1958, and 1962. [59] The rules now in force may therefore be considered as those which have withstood the test of experience.

Oral proceedings are held at the discretion of the presiding member of the Tribunal. Even when one of the parties requests such proceedings, the consent of the presiding member is required. In the oral proceedings, witnesses or experts may be presented and examined. Each party has the right of oral argument and of comment on the evidence given.[60]

If it is desired to bring in witnesses or experts, each party must inform the Executive Secretary in advance and through him, the other party, of the names and descriptions of such witnesses and experts. The points to which the evidence is to refer must also be indicated. The witnesses and experts are examined not only by the Tribunal but by the parties, their representatives or counsel, under the control of the presiding member. Each witness or expert must make the customary oath before giving his evidence.[61]

The Tribunal determines the sequence of oral proceedings. The parties, however, retain the right to comment briefly on any statement to which they have not replied. The Tribunal may exclude evidence which it considers irrelevant, frivolous, or lacking in probative value. It may also limit the oral testimony where it considers the written documentation adequate. The oral proceedings are held in public unless the Tribunal decides that exceptional circumstances call for closed sessions.[62]

The oral proceedings are conducted in one of the working languages of the General Assembly. Each oral statement, whether it has been made by a member of the Tribunal, a party, counsel, a witness, or an expert, is simultaneously translated into English or French as the case may be.[63] The Tribunal President is variously addressed by counsel as "Mr. President," "Your Highness," "Your Honor," and "Mr. Chairman." Counsel address each other as "my opponent," "my friend opposite," "my colleague opposite," or by name.[64]

The Tribunal may at any stage of the proceedings order the production of documents or of such other evidence as may be required. It may arrange for any measures of inquiry as may be necessary.[65] The Tribunal confirmed this power in Judgment No. 81 when it noted that, "in accordance with its Rules, it possesses the broadest powers to request from the parties any documents or information necessary for the consideration of a case." [66]

If the Tribunal finds that the procedure prescribed in the Staff Regulations or Rules has not been observed, it may, at the request of the Secretary-General and prior to the determination of the merits, order the case remanded for institution or correction of the required procedure. In such a case, it may order the payment of compensation to the applicant for loss caused by the procedural delay. If the Secretary-General fails to make a request for a remand within two days of the notification of procedural defects, then the Tribunal proceeds to decide on the substance of the case.[67]

The Tribunal has thus far ordered three cases remanded. In one case, it found defects in the proceedings of the Joint Appeals Board and ordered that "the case should now be the subject of proper and appropriate procedure" through the Board.[68] In another case it concluded that the Review Board failed to observe due process. Thus, without deciding the merits of the case, it decided that the case should be remanded to the Board for reconsideration and further action. At the same time it ordered payment to the applicant of compensation equivalent to three months' net base salary for loss caused by the procedural delay. In this judgment, the Tribunal declared that the choice between deciding the merits of a case and remanding it "is not to be motivated by purely legal considerations; but [that] the practical possibility and the eventual effect of the correction of the procedure required must be taken into account." [69]

The third case concerned termination of a permanent appointment for reasons of health. After examining all the circumstances of the case, the Tribunal concluded that the appropriate procedure of the medical examination of the applicant was not carried out and that, consequently, the former had been denied due process. It ordered that the case be remanded for correction of the procedure and that the applicant be paid as compensation an amount equal to two months' net base salary for the loss caused by the procedural delay. [70]

Any person to whom the Tribunal is open may apply to intervene in a case at any stage of the proceedings on the ground that he has a right which may be affected by the judgment to be given by the Tribunal. An application for such an intervention must be drawn up in accordance with a form prescribed by the Tribunal. If the application is admitted, a copy thereof is transmitted to the parties to the case. Such documents as the President deems fit are in turn transmitted to the intervener by the Executive Secretary. The Tribunal alone can decide on the admissibility of every application for intervention. [71]

The right of intervention is also granted to the Secretary-General, the chief administrative officer of a specialized agency to which the competence of the Tribunal has been extended, and the Chairman of the Joint Staff Pension Board. They must, however, give an advance notice to the President, stating that they consider that their respective administrations may be affected by the judgment to be given by the Tribunal. The Tribunal, furthermore, encourages intervention if it considers that a person may have an interest in such action. [72]

In Judgment No. 1, the Tribunal commented on the right of

intervention. Stressing that the right was granted exclusively to persons who had access to the Tribunal under the Statute and "whose rights may be affected by the judgment," it said:

> Whereas it is reasonable to admit that the decision to be given may, in a general manner, affect the interest which the staff members of the United Nations have in seeing that the contracts of employment and terms of appointment of all staff members are observed by the Administration, nevertheless the contention does not seem admissible that the individual contractual rights of each staff member holding a permanent contract can be directly affected by this decision.[73]

It thus rejected the application for intervention. In an addendum to the same judgment, an application for intervention was sustained on the ground that the applicant was in a position similar to that of the other staff members in the cases in question.[74] No other intervention has been applied for or allowed since then.

The Tribunal may grant a hearing for purposes of information, to persons to whom the Tribunal is open, even though they are not parties to the case. It may also grant a hearing to duly authorized representatives of the staff association of the organization concerned. In either event, the Tribunal has full discretion and must satisfy itself that such persons are likely to furnish information pertinent to the case.[75] The Executive Secretary sends twice a year to all members of the Tribunal copies of all the decisions of the Tribunal during the preceding period. The Tribunal has authority to regulate all other procedural matters which are not expressly provided for in the Rules.[76]

The Tribunal may hold four types of sessions—plenary, special plenary, ordinary, and extraordinary. A plenary session is held once a year, normally during the last quarter of the year, for the purpose of election of officers and any other matters affecting the functioning of the Tribunal. When there are no cases on the list, however, the president, after consulting the other members, may decide to postpone the plenary session to a later date.[77]

A special plenary session is convened by the President when he considers it necessary to deal with a question affecting the operation of the Tribunal. He must notify the members at least thirty days in advance of the date of the opening of such a session. Four members constitute a quorum for plenary sessions. The sessions are normally held at the United Nations Headquarters in New York City; the President may, however, if circumstances require, fix a different place after consultation with the Executive Secretary.[78]

An ordinary session is held each year during the period of the plenary session and in the second quarter of the year for the purpose of considering cases. It is convened by the President only if there are cases on the list which by their number or urgency justify, in his opinion, the holding of the session. He must communicate his decision to members of the Tribunal at least thirty days in advance. The President designates three members, who constitute the Tribunal for the purpose of sitting in each particular case or group of cases. He may also designate one or more members to serve as alternates. Since no case can be heard by the Tribunal except under the chairmanship of the President or one of the Vice-Presidents, one of them is invariably included in the panel for each case.[79]

An extraordinary session may be called by the President if he considers that the number or urgency of the cases on the list requires such a session. He must give the members an advance notice of at least fifteen days. The dates and places for ordinary and extraordinary sessions are set by him after consultation with the Executive Secretary. The latter sends to the members of the Tribunal, designated by the President, the dossiers and other documentation relating to the cases at hand.[80]

The deliberations of the Tribunal are held in private; all decisions are made by a majority vote.[81] The manner in which the judgments are drafted could not be determined at this writing; the judgments, however, must state the reasons on which they are based and are drawn up in any of the five official languages of the United Nations. They must be in two originals which are deposited in the archives of the United Nations Secretariat. A copy of the judgments is communicated to each of the parties to the case. In addition, copies are made available on request to interested persons.[82]

According to Hudson, practice has developed certain standards for the contents of decisions of international tribunals. Hence

a decision should describe the composition of the tribunal; it should trace the initiation and progress of the proceedings and the development of the parties' submissions; it should state the facts presented to the tribunal; it should give an exposition of the law applicable; it should set forth the results reached by the tribunal in applying the law to the facts; and it should close with an operative conclusions (dispositif) which disposes of the issues in the case.[83]

An examination of the judgments rendered by the Tribunal thus far reveals a remarkable conformity with the above standards.

A typical judgment of the Tribunal[84] bears a judgment number and a case number, and lists parties to the case.[85] It then describes the composition of the Tribunal for the case and briefly recounts the initiation and progress of the proceedings. This is followed by a summary of the facts in the case, the applicant's principal contentions, and the respondent's reply. Next comes the Tribunal's judgment, including an exposition of the law applicable and conclusions reached. Finally, an operative conclusion is stated in a clear and concise language.

The practice of allowing the appending of dissenting or separate opinions in judgments, prevalent in common–law tribunals and also followed in the International Court of Justice, is noticeable in the judgments of the Tribunal. In examining fourteen years' jurisprudence, one dissenting opinion, one separate opinion, and sixteen statements (usually expressing concurrence with the decision in the judgment concerned) may be detected.[86] The paucity of disagreements among members of the Tribunal may be explained by the fact that only three members sit in any particular case. That unanimity is relatively easy to seek when the number is so small need not be labored. As is customary in all judicial decisions, the judgments of the Tribunal are signed by the members who have considered the case and by the Executive Secretary.

To summarize, the Tribunal functions in conformity with a procedure prescribed in the Statute and Rules. Thus an applicant must first exhaust the available administrative remedy before he may institute proceedings before the Tribunal. The proceedings are both written and oral and resemble those of national courts. They are, however, characterized by flexibility and informality. The practice of the Tribunal with respect to the form and contents of the judgments is strikingly similar to that followed in other international tribunals, notably the International Court of Justice and its predecessor, the Permanent Court of International Justice.

As a special international tribunal with limited competence, the Tribunal applies and pronounces a body of law which is *sui generis*.[87] Mme. Bastid chooses to call it "le droit administratif interne des Nations Unies relatif aux fonctionnaires." [88] It is neither international law nor municipal law. Nor can it be called administrative law, national or international, in the usual meaning of the term.[89] For the Tribunal is competent to adjust, not any dispute involving administrative action or decision, but only that which relates to employment relations in the United Nations.

However, any tribunal worthy of the name must function within established judicial limitations and must apply law.[90] What are the judicial limitations within which the Tribunal must function? Unlike the Statute of the International Court of Justice, the Statute of the Tribunal is conspicuously silent on this matter. Whereas the former expressly provides for the categories of law to be applied by the Court,[91] the latter merely indicates that the Tribunal is to interpret "contracts" and "terms of appointment" of United Nations staff members, which include "all pertinent regulations and rules in force at the time of alleged nonobservance, including the staff pension regulations." [92] In practical terms, the "internal administrative law of the United Nations" which the Tribunal may apply includes nine categories.[93]

Contracts

As noted, the Statute explicitly states that the Tribunal is competent to pronounce judgments upon application alleging nonobservance of contracts or of the terms of appointment of staff members. It is therefore quite clear that contracts are among the principal legal documents which the Tribunal must interpret and apply. Normally, a letter of appointment and a letter of acceptance constitute the contract of employment. The parties to the contract are the staff member concerned and the Secretary-General, acting on behalf of the Organization as its representative.[94]

The letter of appointment states:

(i) that the appointment is subject to the provisions of the Staff Regulations and of the Staff Rules applicable to the category of appointment in question, and to changes which may be duly made in such regulations and rules from time to time;
(ii) the nature of appointment;
(iii) the date at which the staff member is required to enter upon his duties;
(iv) the period of appointment, the notice required to terminate it and period of probation, if any;
(v) the category, level, commencing rate of salary, and if increments are allowable, the scale of increments and the maximum available;
(vi) any special conditions which may be applicable.[95]

The contract is of public law nature, rather than private. This is evident from the fact that one party to the contract—the Secretary-General acting on behalf of the United Nations—can unilaterally modify the obligations of the other party. In other words, the staff member, by signing the contract, the terms of which have been unilaterally laid down, undertakes to be bound by both the Staff Regulations and Rules. Whereas the former are established by the General Assembly, the latter are unilaterally promulgated by the Secretary-General.[96]

Staff Regulations and Rules

By virtue of Article 2 of the Statute, the Tribunal is called upon to apply the Staff Regulations and Rules. The former set forth broad principles; the latter spell out the details concerning their implementation. The topics they deal with are: *(a)* duties, obligations and privileges; *(b)* classification of posts and staff; *(c)* salaries and related allowances; *(d)* appointment and promotion; *(e)* annual and special leave; *(f)* social security; *(g)* travel and removal expenses; *(h)* staff relations; *(i)* separation from service; *(j)* disciplinary measures; *(k)* appeals, and *(e)* general provisions.[97] The judgments pronounced by the Tribunal are replete with references to and interpretations of the Regulations and Rules. Hence, along with the contracts, these constitute principal legal vehicles of the Tribunal.[98]

Internal Administrative Instructions

Aside from the Staff Regulations and Rules, the Tribunal has applied internal administrative instructions of the Secretariat. Notably, the Administrative Manual,[99] and the Secretary-General's Bulletin have been cited in the judgments of the Tribunal.[100] The Tribunal has declared in one of the judgments:

. . . the contractual relationship between the Secretary-General and the staff is governed not only by the Staff Regulations and Staff Rules, but also by any directives lawfully issued in pursuance thereto by the Secretary-General, the main body of which are to be found in the Administrative Manual. It follows that . . . the Administrative Manual, being binding upon the Administration and the staff, is a document which the Tribunal must apply under the terms of article 2 of its Statute.[101]

It has ruled in another judgment that the Secretary-General's Bulletin, "while of a temporary nature, has the legal force of a provision of the Staff Rules and Regulations, non-observance of which can be pleaded before the Tribunal under article 2 of its Statute." [102]

Resolutions of the General Assembly

In a number of cases, the Tribunal has invoked resolutions of the General Assembly not incorporated in the Staff Regulations or Rules. In one case, it noted that such resolutions, together with the Secretary-General's circulars by which they were put into effect, were, with respect to the staff members to whom they applied, part of the terms of appointment and that, consequently, it was duty bound to take them into account.[103]

Statute and Rules of the Tribunal

It is plain that the Tribunal can and must apply its own Statute and Rules. These indeed are the maps which constantly guide the Tribunal in its legal journey.[104] On various occasions, it has been found necessary to interpret the provisions of the Statute relative to its powers.[105]

Municipal Law

The Tribunal does not exclude the possibility of applying local laws when and if they are considered relevant.[106] It clearly indicated that it was prepared to apply Egyptian labor law in a 1956 case, when it based its inability to proceed to final judgment in the case on the ground, *inter alia*, that: "The relevant local labour laws of Egypt . . . are not before the Tribunal." [107] The Tribunal later ruled that, in accordance with the terms of an Administrative Instruction, the applicant had the right to claim benefits prescribed by Egyptian labor laws.[108] The Tribunal has also had an occasion to refer to the Immigration and Nationality Act (1952) of the United States.[109]

International Law

At least on one occasion, the Tribunal was led to rely on international law. In Judgment No. 64, it invoked "The Hague Convention (No. V) respecting the Rights and Duties of Neutral Powers and Persons in case of War on Land, Article 13 (1907)." In the same judgment it also cited Oppenheim's *International Law*, by Lauterpacht, regarding the legal status of a prisoner of war escaped into neutral territory.[110] From the above it appears that the Tribunal considers itself competent to apply international law if need be.

The Charter of the United Nations, which doubtless forms an integral part of contemporary international law, has been frequently invoked by the parties before the Tribunal, and the latter has given interpretations thereof. The provisions most frequently mentioned are those dealing with the Secretariat, such as Articles 97, 100, and 101. [111] Applicants have also invoked the Universal Declaration of Human Rights.[112] However, the Tribunal has expressed agreement with the respondent's view that general human rights should not be confused with particular conditions of service which govern the employment contract of staff members.[113] In so doing, it has inferentially excluded the possibility of applying the Declaration.

General Principles of Law

Because of lacunae in written laws, the Tribunal is sometimes constrained to resort to what is commonly known as "general principles of law." These refer to those principles which are common to diverse systems of law and which may therefore be regarded as possessing universal validity.[114] The statutes of both the Permanent Court and the International Court have recognized them as applicable law.[115] The possibility of applying international custom, on the other hand, according to Mme. Bastid, is ruled out by the peculiar nature of the problems with which the Tribunal has to deal.[116]

In its judgments, the Tribunal has referred to "the general principles of law," [117] and the "general principles regarding the interpretation of judgments." [118] In Judgment No. 88, it quoted with approval the "generally accepted" principle that, "in the absence of specific provisions to the contrary, the words should be given their normal meaning." [119] In this connection, it may be noted that the Tribunal also draws on its own previous judgments as well as the jurisprudence of other international administrative tribunals. It is a standard practice of the Tribunal to borrow, usually without specific mention, many paragraphs of its previous judgments whenever applicable. It has cited the case-law of the League Tribunal in connection with an award of legal costs.[120] It has also quoted advisory opinions of the International Court of Justice.[121] As for the jurisprudence of the French *Conseil d'Etat*, another spiritual ancestor of the Tribunal, it may be said that although counsel have occasionally mentioned it, the Tribunal itself has thus far failed to make any reference to it. This, according to Mme. Bastid, is partly explained by the fact that with very rare exceptions the Tribunal has always included one or two members of common-law background who are little acquainted with French administrative law.[122]

Equity

The Tribunal has occasionally used the term "equity" in its judgments. In Judgment No. 2 it said that the action of the Secretary-General had been in conflict with "what appear to the Tribunal to be fair and equitable principles of procedure." [123] In Judgment No. 12 it gave consideration to "the equity and justice of equating Applicant's position, as a minimum provision, with that of employees who have been terminated in a manner satisfying the full requirements of the law." [124] In another judgment it referred to "the principle of equity among Member States." [125] On still another occasion, it said:

> . . . the Tribunal considers that rules of equity and justice do require access to documents and information within the exclusive possession of the Administration in so far as it relates to the staff member concerned and is relevant to the proceedings under consideration.[126]

Finally, according to Mme. Bastid, considerations of equity also underlay the Tribunal's decision in Judgment No. 64, even though the Tribunal did not make any explicit statement to that effect.[127] While numerous references have thus been made to the term "equity" by the Tribunal, its precise meaning nevertheless remains to be spelled out. In the broad sense of international law, rather than in the common-law sense, the term has much in common with the general concept of natural justice. It is that vague and undefinable something which blends conscience, reason, good faith, and natural justice.[128]

In short, the law that can be applied by the Tribunal is both diverse and complex. It can apply a body of law which may be characterized as the internal administrative law of the United Nations. This includes contracts of staff members, the Staff Regulations and Rules, administrative instructions, and resolutions of the General Assembly; naturally, it can and must apply its own Statute and Rules. In addition, references have sometimes been made to municipal and international laws. The so-called general principles of law have also been recognized in the Tribunal's jurisprudence. Finally, the Tribunal has drawn on equity, when law is silent or obscure.

A question closely related to that of the law applicable by the Tribunal is: what are the rules of interpretation that the Tribunal follows? In its own words:

. . . the construction of a rule or regulation must respond to the following requirements: (1) the interpretation must be a logical one; (2) it must be based upon an attempt to understand both the letter and the spirit of the rule under construction; and (3) the interpretation must be in conformity with the context of the body of rules and regulations to which it belongs, and must seek to give the maximum effect to these rules and

The Tribunal often examines or refers to the *travaux preparatoires* in interpreting the intent and meaning of specific regulations.[130] It is also guided by the statements of the International Court of Justice that "the first duty of a tribunal which is called upon to interpret and apply the provisions [of a legal text] is to endeavour to give effect to them in their natural and ordinary meaning in the context in which they occur," and "It is a cardinal principle of interpretation that words must be interpreted in the sense which they would normally have in their context, unless such interpretation would lead to something unreasonable or absurd." [131]

In the final analysis, the practical significance of the Tribunal is contingent upon the effectiveness of the remedies which it affords. For only when it tangibly remedies the wrong that has been done to staff members, can it inspire the latter's confidence and boost their morale. One of the major purposes in establishing the Tribunal, it may be recalled, was to provide adequate legal protection for the rights of staff members, thereby strengthening their sense of security—a condition which was felt to be indispensable for the development of a competent international civil service.

In designing the blueprint, however, the architects of the Tribunal were painfully aware that a delicate balance must be struck between two competing needs if the Tribunal was fully to serve its purposes: they were aware that the sense of security could not be had at any price but must be balanced by the requirement for an efficient administration. This latter called for the unhampered exercise of discretion on the part of the Secretary-General in matters relating to the internal administration of the Secretariat.

These considerations underlay the decision to allow some flexibility in the kinds of remedies that would be available from the Tribunal. Simply stated, either the administrative decision contested is reversed, or the applicant is paid compensation in lieu of the reversal. The course of action to be taken is left, not to the judgment of the Tribunal, but to the discretion of the Secretary-General.

Since the decision contested may involve either action or inaction—the applicant may object to either what the Secretary-General has done or what he has failed to do—its reversal may take either of these two forms: the rescinding of the decision contested or the specific performance of the obligations invoked.[132] Thus the Tribunal may order the Secretary-General to reinstate a staff member whom he has dismissed, on the ground that his action had infringed the staff member's contractual rights, or it may order him to grant a staff member a home leave with pay on the basis of an obligation he has previously assumed. Such a judgment is contingent upon the Tribunal's finding that the application is well founded. Otherwise, it simply rejects the application as without ground, in which case, the decision contested stands.

In spite of the Tribunal's order to the above effect, the Secretary-General may adhere to his original decision if he considers that to reverse his decision would be contrary to the interest of the United Nations. In anticipation of such a possibility, the Tribunal must fix, at the time of judgment, the amount of compensation to be paid to the applicant for the injury sustained. The amount of such compensation must not normally exceed the equivalent of two years' net base salary of the applicant. The Tribunal, however, may exceed that limit if exceptional circumstances justify such a course of action.[133]

In determining the degree of the injury suffered in specific cases, the Tribunal must consider:

to what extent the Applicant has expectation of continued employment, taking into account the terms and nature of the contract, the Staff Rules and Regulations and the facts pertaining to the situation and must evaluate the Applicant's chances of earning a livelihood after separation from the United Nations.[134]

In one case, it declared that the applicant's claims based upon the prospect of continued employment by the United Nations until retirement were unacceptable because he "has attempted to value . . . a problematical chance, rather than anything approaching a firm expectancy." It quoted a passage from McCormick's *Handbook on the Law of Damages* which read: "Where the damage claimed by the plaintiff is the deprivation of an opportunity (not amounting to a reasonable certainty) to gain a specific prize, award, or profit, the courts have been slow to allow recovery of the value of a mere chance." [135]

The conferring of leeway to the Secretary-General, noted above, motivated as it was by the concern for managerial efficiency, had an unfortunate effect, which was not totally unforeseen. In practice, it was tantamount to giving the Secretary-General the power to override the judgments of the Tribunal. For he can consistently refuse to carry out its decisions by invoking the infinitely plastic clause, "in the interest of the United Nations." This is not merely a possibility but what has actually happened.

It may be recalled, in this connection, that during the 1949 debate over the draft statute of the Tribunal in the Fifth Committee some delegations pointed out that the character of the Tribunal would be seriously compromised if the Secretary-General were allowed to modify its judgments in the above manner. The Tribunal, they warned, would not, in that event, be concerned with redressing injustice but would simply pay compensation.[136] The Statute which was finally adopted by the General Assembly, however, retained the provision that the Secretary-General would have the option of either complying with the Tribunal's original judgment or paying compensation in lieu thereof. Article 9 read in part, ". . . but if, in exceptional circumstances, such rescinding or specific performance is, in the opinion of the Secretary-General, impossible or inadvisable, the Tribunal shall within a period of not more than sixty days order the payment to the applicant of compensation for the injury sustained."

It was hoped that the qualifying clause, "in exceptional circumstances," would act as a brake on the Secretary-General's decisions. That hope, however, was but short-lived. For, after four years of experimentation with the Tribunal, the late Dag Hammarskjöld, then Secretary-General, reported:

Experience has indicated that, particularly in cases involving termination of appointment, where the Tribunal finds that the application is well founded, *the payment of compensation should be the rule rather than the exception.* It is normally not in keeping with the interest of good administration to reinstate an employee whom the Secretary-General has considered it necessary to terminate. At the same time, from the point of view of the staff member, it is not desirable to require a new finding that reinstatement is "impossible or inadvisable." Administrative experience and considerations indicate that the normal reaction, in case a decision of the Secretary-

General is not upheld by the Administrative Tribunal, should be the payment of compensation. In those circumstances, however, where the Secretary-General believes that it would not be disadvantageous to rescind his decision, he should have the option of offering such rescission to the applicant in lieu of the compensation ordered.[137]

He further pointed out that it was desirable, from the point of view of financial administration, to place a limit on the compensation. Finally, he felt that in cases where the decision contested stemmed from procedural, rather than substantive, defects, the Secretary-General should be given an opportunity to correct such defects as might exist. In that case, he added, the United Nations should of course be required to pay compensation for any loss sustained by the applicant. He therefore proposed an amendment to Article 9 of the Statute then in force. The amendment would make the payment of compensation the rule rather than the exception; place a ceiling on the amount of compensation which might be awarded; and provide for the remanding of a case where procedural defects were found.[138]

Hammarskjöld's proposals set off a lengthy debate in the Fifth Committee. The reaction of the Staff Council, as might have been expected, was cool. The Council stressed that "the usual remedy in a case in which the Tribunal finds in favour of the applicant should be the rescinding of the decision contested or the specific performance of the obligation invoked." It was equally hostile to the idea of limiting the amount of compensation to two years' net base salary. It said: "it would seem better to leave the Tribunal gradually to develop standards for assessing the injury sustained, than to establish arbitrarily a limit which might, in a case of wrongful dismissal causing special hardship, preclude fair and reasonable compensation . . . ." [139]

The views expressed by various delegations in the course of the debate were mixed. Some delegations were opposed to such an amendment, because it might alter the existing balance between the power of the Secretary-General and of the Tribunal. They pointed out that, in many national administrations, reinstatement was the normal, not exceptional, remedy and that compensation was not a satisfactory substitute for the loss of employment. Others, while agreeing that compensation should be the rule, objected to a rigid ceiling thereon. They thought that to impose such a ceiling would be tantamount to reducing the Tribunal to a body whose sole function would be to approve or disapprove the grant of previously determined indemnities.[140]

It was finally decided to retain the original idea of making rescission or performance the rule and allowing compensation in lieu thereof only in exceptional circumstances. The phrase, "in the interest of the United Nations," however, was introduced so as to strengthen the point that the paramount consideration should always be effective functioning of the Organization. Meanwhile, the proposed ceiling on the amount of compensation, together with the procedure for remanding, was accepted.[141]

Nevertheless, the total effect is such that the Secretary-General is still completely protected against the possibility of having to reverse his decision against his will. Conversely, the staff member is precluded, for all practical purposes, from having his grievances redressed even if they are justified; the only satisfaction that may be forthcoming is monetary compensation.

The judgments of the Tribunal are final and without appeal.[142] This statement, however, should not be taken literally; the Statute also provides for the possibility both of revision and of review of judgments. The Secretary-General or the applicant may apply to the Tribunal for a revision of a judgment if the following conditions are met: the discovery of some fact of such a nature as to be a decisive factor; the fact must have been unknown both to the Tribunal and to the party claiming revision at the time of the judgment in question; and such ignorance must not be attributable to negligence. The application must be made within thirty days of the discovery of the fact and within one year of the date of the judgment. In addition, the Tribunal may, either *proprio motu* or on the application of any of the parties, correct at any time clerical or arithmetical mistakes in judgments or errors arising therein from any accidental slip or omission.[143]

The amount of compensation fixed by the Tribunal in a previous judgment was thus amended in Judgment No. 51, after the Tribunal found that the age and date of birth of the applicant had been erroneously recorded in the relevant documents. The Secretary-General had initiated the motion for the revision.[144] In a later judgment, an application for revision filed by a staff member was rejected on the ground that neither a discovery of new fact nor a clerical or arithmetical error affording competence to the Tribunal to revise its decision existed. The Tribunal made it clear that the powers of revision "are strictly limited by the Statute of the Administrative Tribunal and cannot be enlarged or abridged in the exercise of its jurisdiction by the Tribunal." [145]

The judgments of the Tribunal may be reviewed by the International Court of Justice under a procedure laid down in a 1955 amendment to the Statute. The revision procedure described above was also established by the same amendment. The Court's competence, however, is confined to giving an advisory opinion as to whether the Tribunal has committed procedural and/or substantive errors, thereby occasioning a failure of justice. The procedure, together with the background for its adoption, is more fully described below.

The General Assembly in a resolution of December 17, 1954 accepted, in principle, judicial review of the judgments of the Tribunal. A Special Committee on Review of Administrative Tribunal Judgments was established pursuant to that resolution. The Special Committee, after considering the problem, recommended an addition of two new articles to the Statute. One of the proposed articles, namely, article 12, dealt with revision of the Tribunal's judgments—a topic already examined; the other article, i.e., article 11, spelled out a review procedure whereby the International Court of Justice would be vested with a quasi-appellate competence over the Tribunal's judgments.[146]

Specifically, the proposed new article 11 envisaged the establishment of a special committee composed of member states the representatives of which had served on the General Committee of the most recent regular session of the General Assembly. The General Committee is composed of the President and Thirteen Vice-Presidents of the General Assembly and the chairmen of the seven Main Committees. All these are elected at the beginning of each session of the General Assembly. The General Committee serves as a kind of steering committee for the Assembly. A member state, the Secretary-General, or a person in respect of whom a judgment had been rendered by the Tribunal might make an application to the committee to request an advisory opinion of the International Court of Justice on one or more of the following grounds: the Tribunal had exceeded its jurisdiction or competence, or had erred on a question of law relating to the provisions of the Charter, or had committed a fundamental error in procedure.

If the committee decided that there was a substantial basis for the application, it should request an advisory opinion of the Court.[147]

In the event of a negative finding by the Committee or if no decision is taken within prescribed periods, the judgment of the Tribunal should become final. When the Court had given an advisory opinion pursuant to a request, the Secretary-General should either give effect to the opinion of the Court or request the Tribunal to convene specially in order that it might confirm its original judgment, or render a new judgment, in conformity with the opinion of the Court. In order to protect the interest of a staff member in whose favor compensation had been requested in an advisory opinion, the Secretary-General, if he deemed it necessary, should make an advance payment to him of one-third of the amount awarded, less such termination benefits as had already been paid.[148]

The Fifth Committee examined the above proposals of the Special Committee, along with the views of the Secretary-General, of member states and specialized agencies, and of the Staff Council. Recalling that at no time had he felt the need for a review procedure for normal cases coming before the Tribunal, the Secretary-General stressed that the following principles were essential to a sound development of the administrative and legal system of the United Nations:

1. The review should serve only as an outlet in exceptional cases and should not be for regular use;
2. The review should be truly judicial in character, the tribunal should be a permanent body and its members should have the highest qualifications and stature;
3. The review should be expeditious and not result in undue complications or delay;
4. The applicant should have the right to initiate the review and to participate on an equitable basis in any review procedure to be established.[149]

These principles, he noted, had received considerable general support in the Special Committee and were also supported by the Staff Council. Hammarskjöld also foresaw the problem of inequality of parties before the Court—in view of the fact that individuals had no *locus standi* before the Court—and promised to work out a solution. He said he would consider it his responsibility to assure as far as possible an equality of rights for the staff member concerned. He would waive any right which he had to further participate in the proceedings before the Court from which the staff member was excluded except as the Court might specifically require further information. He expressed the hope that member states would exercise a similar restraint and would forego an appearance before the Court in oral proceedings which could not be granted to the staff member.[150]

In a draft resolution proposed jointly by Argentina, Canada, China, Cuba, Iraq, Pakistan, the United Kingdom, and the United States at the opening of the general discussion in the Fifth Committee, the proposals of the Special Committee were recommended for adoption, together with the principle that member states and the Secretary-General should not make oral statements before the Court in any proceedings under the new article 11 of the Statute. Even though, as noted, there were two articles to be considered, discussion in the Fifth Committee centered primarily on the proposed article 11. Principal points raised in the debate, which lasted from October 17–31, 1955, are worthy of note.[151]

The supporters of article 11 argued, first of all, that experience had shown a need for some method of review of the Tribunal's judgments. They further pointed out that the proposed procedure was based on the precedent set by the I.L.O. Tribunal. Since a number of specialized agencies had accepted the jurisdiction of the I.L.O. Tribunal, the members of the United Nations were in the position of having already recognized the precedent. They stressed the fact that the new draft article was intended to limit review to exceptional cases. Two of the grounds for review—questions of competence and of fundamental error in procedure—were identical with those provided for in the Statute of the I.L.O. Tribunal. One additional ground was errors on "a question of law relating to the provisions of the Charter." These grounds, they said, were of such a fundamental nature that they could not be ignored in the interest of justice.[152]

Concerning the controversial issue of allowing a member state to make applications for review, it was pointed out that a member state had a legitimate interest in ensuring the proper application of the Charter and the Staff Regulations, as well as a financial interest in the matter. Furthermore, a state would not have the authority to institute review but only to make an application to a screening committee which would decide whether or not an advisory opinion should be requested from the Court. The supporters of the draft proposals made it clear that the function of the screening committee was only to decide whether or not there was a substantial basis for the application. Its duties would be strictly confined to ascertaining whether there was a genuine application within the specified scope of review. This again was based on the practice of the I.L.O. Tribunal. As the membership of the screening committee would be based on that of the most recently elected General Committee, not only would equitable geographical representation be ensured, but the cumbersome procedure of special elections would also be obviated. Some members expressed the hope that states members of the screening committee should appoint either jurists or administrative experts.[153]

The Court, it was pointed out, was selected as an organ to decide on substantive legal issues because it was an independent, impartial judicial body of the highest standing. It was also consistent with Article 96 of the Charter for authorized organs of the United Nations to request advisory opinions upon legal questions to the Court. As only exceptional cases would come to the Court, it would not be overburdened with trivial cases. Further, it would be neither necessary nor economically justifiable to set up a new appellate machinery. As for the inequality of parties, the supporters of the proposals believed that the draft article 11 included an adequate solution. Under the proposed article the Secretary-General must arrange to transmit to the Court the views of the individual concerned. It was intended that written requests and replies of the individuals concerned would be laid before the Court on a completely equal footing with those of the Secretary-General and member states. Some representatives further pointed out that the Court itself would be a guardian of due process and would not give an opinion if it considered that one of the parties was at a disadvantage.[154]

On the other hand, the opponents of the proposed new article argued that there was no need for a review of the Tribunal's judgments. Neither the Secretary-General nor the Staff Council, they pointed out, had requested the establishment of a review procedure. They underscored the fact that as there were already a number of stages through which a case went before it reached the Tribunal, the latter was in effect a court of appeal. They further stated that the expense, delay, and the constitutional and practical difficulties involved rendered it undesirable to have a review procedure which might also impair the prestige of the Tribunal.[155]

Some representatives objected to the scope of review, stressing particularly that the provision concerning "a question of law relating to the provisions of the Charter" was ambiguous and allowed the possibility of review on almost any question. Objections were further raised as to the right of a member state to make an application for review, the composition of the screening committee, and the use of the advisory proceedings of the Court. The right of a member country to make an application was criticized on the ground that in a truly judicial review only the parties should have a right of initiating the review. The composition of the screening committee, it was argued, introduced a political element into the review, since its membership was based on that of the General Committee which was a political organ of the General Assembly. A staff member, furthermore, would be in a position of inequality before the screening committee, since the member state making an application might in some cases be a member of the committee.[156]

The opponents of the review procedure also considered that the Court was not an appropriate organ for reviewing the Tribunal's judgments. It was doubtful whether such a procedure would be consistent with Article 34 of the Court's Statute which limited the latter's contentious jurisdiction to disputes between States. Moreover, it was somewhat anomalous that advisory opinions of the Court should legally affect the judgments of the Tribunal which were binding. It was also believed that there would be an inherent inequality between the staff member on the one hand and the Secretary-General and member states on the other. An expression of hope by the General Assembly that member states and the Secretary-General would forego their right to an oral hearing would not be a sufficient guarantee. As long as the staff member could not make a personal appearance before the Court, an essential feature of due process of law was lacking. Finally, the proposed procedure was unduly cumbersome and lengthy and would involve additional expense. It might have seriously adverse effects on the stature of international civil servants and on the existing judicial safeguards for the staff.[157]

After lengthy discussions, during which India and Australia, respectively, submitted further amendments, the Fifth Committee finally approved the revised joint draft resolution as a whole, with some amendments. The draft resolution was adopted by the General Assembly on November 8, 1955 with minor drafting changes.[158]

Three classes of persons have the right to make an application for review: (1) a member state, (2) the Secretary-General, and (3) the person in respect of whom a judgment has been rendered by the Tribunal, or his successor *mortis causa*. The grounds for review are four: (1) that the Tribunal has exceeded its jurisdiction or competence; (2) that the Tribunal has failed to exercise jurisdiction vested in it; (3) that the Tribunal has erred on a question of law relating to the provisions of the Charter; (4) that the Tribunal has committed a fundamental error in procedure which has occasioned a failure of justice. A written application invoking one or more of the above grounds may be filed with an unofficial screening committee within thirty days from the date of the judgment. Such an application asks the Committee to request an advisory opinion of the International Court of Justice. The committee, officially called the Committee on Applications for Review of Administrative Tribunal Judgments, is composed of member states, the representatives of which have served on the General Committee of the most recent regular session of the General Assembly.[159]

Within thirty days from the receipt of an application, the Committee must decide whether or not there is a substantial basis for the application. In the event of an affirmative decision, the Committee must request an advisory opinion of the Court. The Secretary-General is responsible for making arrangements for transmitting to the Court the views of the staff member concerned. If no application for review is made by any of those who are entitled to do so or if a decision to request an advisory opinion has not been taken by the Committee within thirty days from the receipt of the application, the judgment of the Tribunal becomes final.[160]

After the Court has given its advisory opinion, the Secretary-General must either give effect to the opinion or request the Tribunal to convene specially in order that it may confirm its original judgment, or give a new judgment, in conformity with the Court's opinion. If not requested to convene, the Tribunal at its next session either confirms its judgment or brings it into conformity with the advisory opinion. If award of compensation has been made by the Tribunal in favor of the person concerned and the Committee has requested an advisory opinion, the Secretary-General may make an advance payment to him of one-third of the total amount of compensation awarded by the Tribunal less such termination benefits as have already been paid. The Secretary-General, however, must first satisfy himself that such a person will otherwise be handicapped in protecting his interests and may make the payment within fifteen days of the decision to request an advisory opinion. The staff member must pay back to the United Nations the amount, if any, by which the advance payment exceeds any sum to which he is entitled in accordance with the opinion of the Court.[161]

The Committee on Application for Review of Administrative Tribunal Judgments first convened on October 16, 1956, to consider one application. Having found that there was no substantial basis for the request, it decided not to request an advisory opinion from the Court.[162] In subsequent years, the Committee considered five more applications, of which four were found to lack substantial basis and one did not observe the prescribed time limit; none of them, consequently, went to the Court.[163]

CHAPTER 5

THE JURISPRUDENCE

THE EFFECTIVENESS OF a judicial mechanism such as the Tribunal can best be gauged in terms of both the quantity and quality of judicial business it actually conducts.

Although the importance of judicial statistics as an index of the uses and limits of a tribunal is reasonably clear, one must nevertheless guard against the danger of exaggerating it. As Sydney D. Bailey points out: "The value of a judicial system cannot be judged simply by counting the number of times it is overtly resorted to."[1] Referring to the International Court of Justice, Bailey argues that its usefulness should be determined primarily by "the wrongs that were not done and the disputes that were not allowed to fester simply because the Court existed," and only secondarily by its judicial statistics.[2]

While the Tribunal's utility as a psychological deterrent of arbitrary actions by the Secretary-General is difficult, if not impossible, to prove empirically, Bailey's thesis is sufficiently plausible and thought-provoking; at least, it suggests the wisdom of appreciating the limits of numerical indices in appraising the performance of the Tribunal. With this limitation in mind, we shall first deal briefly with the quantitative method in legal analysis in general and then with some of the pertinent judicial statistics of the Tribunal.

The use of quantitative method in judicial research is a relatively recent phenomenon. Its potential as a useful analytical tool is demonstrated by Glendon Schubert in his recent bibliographical essay on "Behavioral Research in Public Law."[3] Schubert has documented an impressive array of both theoretical and empirical research in what he calls "the analysis of judicial decision-making" conducted during the past half dozen years or so. His four main categories of the research are indicative of the heavy behavioral accent and orientation: (1) group interaction, (2) courts as small groups, (3) the political socialization of judges, and (4) the social psychology of judicial attitudes.

In broad terms, the student of judicial behavior is concerned with the political and social-psychological determinants of judicial decision-making and their mutual interaction. Why does a Supreme Court justice vote in a particular manner in a given case? What factors influence his decision so to vote? Does he vote consistently with respect to the same legal issue? With whom has he sided in voting for or against a case or a group of cases? And why? These are some of the questions which the student of judicial behavior seeks to answer. In so doing, he uses various statistical techniques widely utilized in behavioral science research.

One of the earliest exponents of this approach meriting a special mention is C. Herman Pritchett. Pritchett in two successive volumes, namely, *The Roosevelt Court: A Study in Judicial Politics and Values, 1937–1947* [4] and *Civil Liberties and the Vinson Court,*[5] analyzed the voting behavior of Supreme Court justices using the so-called bloc analysis. Another noteworthy volume is Schubert's work on *Quantitative Analysis of Judicial Behavior.*[6] He expounds four principal methods: the analysis of summary judicial power, bloc analysis, game analysis, and scalogram analysis.

Whatever the intrinsic merit of the above methods, the possibility of applying any of them to the Tribunal is eliminated by the near absence of dissenting or separate opinions in its judgments thus far. As already noted, there exist only one dissenting opinion and one separate opinion in the fourteen years' jurisprudence here examined. More pertinent to the analysis of the Tribunal is an approach employed by Robert V. Presthus and Sevda Erem in their *Statistical Analysis in Comparative Administration: The Turkish Conseil d'Etat.*[7] Presthus and Erem have analyzed a sample of 2,131 cases handled by the Turkish *Conseil d'Etat.* The sample was randomly selected from a universe of 87,640 cases. By using the simple device of counting and comparing such items as types, distribution, and disposition of cases, parties to the case, and geographical origin of cases, they have attempted to arrive at some tentative generalizations about the effectiveness as well as shortcomings of the Turkish system of administrative law as evidenced by the *Conseil d'Etat*.

The Tribunal lends itself to a similar, if more manageable, analysis: we have a universe of ninety judgments and thus may examine the whole universe, rather than a sample. Moreover, the very paucity of judgments further simplifies any counting operation: there are but a few items which may be counted with profit. These are the distribution of judgments, the types of disputes, the nature of judgments, the nature of awards favorable to the applicants, and, finally, the reasons given for the rejection of applications.

In the 14–year period, 1950–63, the Tribunal delivered ninety judgments. The number of judgments and the number of cases handled by the Tribunal do not necessarily match. This is because the Tribunal frequently has not only given more than one judgment with respect to a single dispute but has occasionally disposed of several, rather than one, applications in a single judgment. Thus we find that at the end of 1963 the Tribunal had pronounced ninety judgments, but it had actually dealt with eighty-eight applications.

As Table 2 shows, the busiest year for the Tribunal was 1953, when thirty-four judgments were handed down. This was the year in which the celebrated "political" cases were handled by the Tribunal. The year 1960, on the other hand, saw but a single case adjudged by the Tribunal. On the whole the Tribunal has delivered an average of more than six judgments a year. This is a telling evidence that the continued existence of the Tribunal is both justified and desirable.

The most common types of disputes, as Table 3 indicates, have to do with termination of contracts, i.e., separation from the United Nations service. Disputes concerning termination of probationary, temporary-indefinite, and permanent contracts; non-renewal of fixed-term contracts; and termination of area staff members and of mission appointment thus accounted for more than 66 percent of the Tribunal's judicial business over fourteen years. About 23 percent of disputes have involved (1) requests for rescission of administrative decisions; (2) compensation for injury; (3) claim of damages resulting from a decision not to reinstate a staff member; (4) payment of salary, indemnities, and

Table 2

Year	Frequency
1950	3
1951	9
1952	5
1953	34
1954	5
1955	6
1956	5
1957	3
1958	5
1959	5
1960	1
1961	2
1962	3
1963	4
Total	90

costs; (5) reimbursement of U.S. taxes on UN salaries and on awards in lieu of reinstatement; and (6) alleged nonobservance of terms of employment.

The remainder of disputes is spread over such diverse issues as payment of dependency allowances; denial of due process prior to the proceedings of the Joint Disciplinary Committee; denial of the right to sign waiver of privileges and immunities in order to acquire a permanent residence status in host country; change of administrative status; declaration of inadmissibility on grounds of being frivolous; intervention; interlocutory order; and revision of judgments.

It is evident that the greatest single source of employment disputes in the United Nations is none other than the involuntary termination of employment itself. Significant, however, is the fact that of the disputes involving termination only one-fourth has to do with permanent contracts. This means that most termination disputes originate from those who have been temporarily hired by the Organization in the first place and, consequently, whose termination may be said to have been more or less fore-

Table 3

TYPES OF DISPUTES

1950–1963, INCLUSIVE

Issue in Dispute (1)	Frequency (2)	Percentage (3)
Termination of temporary-indefinite contracts........	31	33.3
Termination of permanent contracts............	16	17.2
Nonrenewal of fixed-term contracts............	9	9.7
Rescission of administrative decisions..................	8	8.6
Compensation for injury.......................	4	4.3
Termination of area staff members.....................	3	3.2
Payment of salary, indemnities, and costs............	3	3.2
Nonobservance of terms of employment..............	3	3.2
Termination of mission appointment..................	2	2.1
Claim of damages resulting from decision not to reinstate...............	2	2.1
Reimbursement of US taxes on UN salaries and awards in lieu of reinstatement..................	2	2.1
Reimbursement of US social security tax on UN salaries...........	1	1.1
Termination of probationary appointment...........	1	1.1
Payment of dependency allowances....................	1	1.1
Denial of due process prior to the proceedings of Disciplinary Committee...........	1	1.1
Denial of right to sign waiver of privileges and immunities...............................	1	1.1
Change of administrative status........................	1	1.1
Declaration of inadmissibility on grounds of being frivolous.............................	1	1.1
Intervention.......................	1	1.1
Interlocutory order.............................	1	1.1
Revision of judgment.........................	1	1.1
Total	93[a]	100.0

[a]Since some cases involve more than one issue, the total exceeds the number of judgments, which is 90.

seen. What is more, whereas 75 percent of the disputes involving termination of permanent contracts have been resolved in favor of the applicants, an equally large proportion of those involving temporary appointments has been settled in favor of the respondent. Note, for example, that about 77 percent each of termination of temporary-indefinite contracts and of nonrenewal

Table 3—*Continued*

Application Sustained (4)	Percentage (5)[b]	Application Rejected (6)	Percentage (7)[c]	Others[d] (8)	Percentage (9)
5	16.1	24	77.4	2	6.4
12	75.0	3	18.7	1	6.2
1	11.1	7	77.7	1	11.1
8	100.0	....	....	....	....
4	100.0	....	....	....	....
....	....	1	33.3	2	66.6
2	66.6	....	....	1	33.3
2	66.6	....	....	1	33.3
....	....	1	50.0	1	50.0
2	100.0	....	....	....	....
....	....	1	50.0	1	50.0
....	....	1	100.0	....	....
....	....	1	100.0	....	....
....	....	1	100.0	....	....
....	....	1	100.0	....	....
....	....	1	100.0	....	....
....	....	1	100.0	....	....
....	....	1	100.0	....	....
1	100.0	....	....	....	....
....	....	1	100.0	....	....
....	....	1	100.0	....	....
37		46		10	

[b] (4) X 100/(2)

[c] (6) X 100/(2)

[d] These include: the remand of a case; the postponement of decision on merits; the revision of a previous judgment; the interpretation of a previous judgment; statements on procedure or legal issues; and the fixing of legal costs.

of fixed-term contracts have been upheld. On the basis of the above statistics, it may be said that to permanent contract holders the United Nations offers a marked stability of employment.

Decisions of the Tribunal embodied in its judgments may be divided into eight categories: (1) the rejection of an application; (2) a finding that the application is well founded; (3) the remand of a case; (4) the postponement of decision on merit; (5) statements on procedure or legal issues; (6) the interpretation of a previous judgment; (7) the revision of a previous judgment; and (8) the fixing of the amount of legal costs. The above list, as is evident from Table 4, is in the order of the frequency with which each item has appeared in the past.

Forty-five judgments, or 50 percent of the total, have rejected applications as being without ground, thus upholding the decision, action, or inaction of the Secretary-General contested. About 35 percent of the judgments, on the other hand, have been in favor of the applicants. This suggests that the Tribunal has conscientiously fulfilled its function as an impartial adjudicator of personnel disputes in the United Nations: neither has it been excessively concerned with the protection of the interests and rights of the international civil servant at the expense of the Organization, nor has it sought to safeguard the interest of the

Table 4

NATURE OF JUDGMENTS

1950–1963, INCLUSIVE

Nature	Frequency	Percentage
Application rejected[a]	45	50.0
Application sustained[b]	32	35.5
Case remanded[c]	3	3.3
Decision on merits postponed	3	3.3
Statement on procedure or legal issue	3	3.3
Interpretation of a previous judgment	2	2.2
Revision of a previous judgment	1	1.1
Amount of legal costs fixed	1	1.1
Total	90	99.9[d]

[a]Complaints of the applicant are found to be without ground.

[b]Complaints of the applicant are found justified; the Tribunal orders the rescinding of the decision contested, or the specific performance of the obligation invoked, or compensation in lieu of the above.

[c]The Tribunal finds procedural deficiency and orders the Secretary-General to institute or correct the required procedure.

[d]Less than 100 due to fractions in computation.

Organization without regard to the rights of its staff members. These two are not mutually exclusive but reconcilable. The Tribunal was created to see that reconciliation is attained in a just and equitable manner and to the maximum benefit of both the Organization and its staff members. The record of its performance thus far appears to warrant the tentative conclusion that the Tribunal has not shattered the original expectation of its creators. A more definitive judgment on this matter, however, must await further analysis.

As already noted, the only effective remedy of which the Tribunal is capable appears to be monetary compensation. Thus we see from Table 5 that nearly 78 percent of awards favorable to applicants have been awards of arrears of salary, of compensation for injury or in lieu of reinstatement, of costs, of entitlement for home leave, and of termination indemnity. The remainder consists of rescission of termination, rescission of administrative decisions, and decision on place of entitlement for home leave. Of these the rescission of termination has invariably been substituted by the award of compensation in lieu of reinstatement—an option granted to the Secretary-General under Article 9, para-

Table 5

NATURE OF AWARDS FAVORABLE TO APPLICANTS,
1950–1963, INCLUSIVE

Description of Awards	Frequency	Percentage
Award of arrears in salary	26	27.3
Award of compensation for injury or in lieu of reinstatement	25	26.3
Award of legal costs	21	22.1
Rescission of termination	14	14.7
Rescission of administrative decision	6	6.3
Award of entitlement for home leave	1	1.0
Award of termination indemnity	1	1.0
Decision on place of entitlement for home leave	1	1.0
Total	95[a]	99.7[b]

[a]A judgment favorable to the applicant frequently contains more than one award; thus, while there are only 32 judgments in the applicants' favor, one can count as many as 95 awards within the 32 judgments.

[b]Less than 100 due to fractions in computation.

graph 1, of the Statute. This brings the proportion of monetary awards to more than 92 percent. Under these circumstances, the accusation that the Tribunal does not really redress injustice but merely pays compensation appears to have a considerable amount of truth in it.

Table 6

REASONS GIVEN FOR THE REJECTION OF APPLICATIONS, 1950-1963, INCLUSIVE

Reasons Given	Frequency	Percentage
Absence of evidence establishing improper motivation for the contested decision	26	32.1
Validity of the grounds for termination	18	22.2
Incompetence of the Tribunal to deal with internal administrative matters	13	16.0
Absence of any procedural irregularity	7	8.6
Proper exercise of discretionary powers by the Secretary-General	5	6.1
Absence of any legal reason for reviewing the contested decision	4	4.9
Absence of expectancies of renewal of the contract	1	1.2
Right of the Secretary-General to dismiss for serious misconduct	1	1.2
Incompetence of the Tribunal to deal with subject matter	1	1.2
Incompetence of the Tribunal to consider a claim not previously submitted to the Joint Disciplinary Committee	1	1.2
Incompetence of the Tribunal to express views on the accuracy of the diagnoses or conclusions of the medical profession	1	1.2
Failure of the applicant to observe prescribed procedure	1	1.2
Absence of evidence establishing that the applicant's illness was service incurred	1	1.2
Absence of legal grounds for the revision of judgment	1	1.2
Total	81[a]	99.5[b]

[a]The discrepancy between this figure and the number of applications rejected, which is 45, is attributable to the fact that the Tribunal frequently cites more than one ground for the rejection of each application.

[b]Less than 100 due to fractions in computation.

The reasons most frequently given by the Tribunal for the rejection of application, as Table 6 shows, are: (1) absence of evidence establishing improper motivation for the contested decision; (2) the validity of the grounds for termination; and (3) the incompetence of the Tribunal to deal with purely internal administrative matters; (4) absence of any procedural irregularity; (5) the proper exercise of discretionary powers by the Secretary-General; and (6) absence of any legal reason for reviewing the contested decision.

Other reasons cited include: absence of expectancies of renewal of the contract; the right of the Secretary-General to dismiss a staff member for serious misconduct; the incompetence of the Tribunal to deal with the subject matter of the dispute; the incompetence of the Tribunal to express views on the accuracy of the diagnoses or conclusions of the medical profession; failure of the applicant to observe prescribed procedure; absence of evidence establishing that the applicant's illness was service-incurred; and absence of legal grounds for the revision of judgment.

Often more than one of the above grounds has been cited in a single judgment. An examination of the six most frequently cited grounds reveals that the decisions of the Secretary-General tend to be upheld as long as they are not improperly motivated, i.e., not attributable to personal biases against the applicant concerned, but based on objective and impersonal criteria, and as long as they pertain to internal administrative matters, matters which properly belong to the discretionary domain of the Secretary-General. The boundaries of the above domain will be more clearly delineated in the following pages.

The above analysis of the judicial statistics of the Tribunal, in and of itself, is a manifestly inadequate introduction to the jurisprudence of the Tribunal; it must be supplemented, enlarged, and clarified by the exposition of its substantive, as opposed to numerical and topical, contents. A useful approach for this purpose is suggested by Sir Gerald G. Fitzmaurice. In a series of articles in *The British Year Book of International Law*, he ably expounded the principles of law embodied in the jurisprudence of the International Court of Justice up to 1959. [8] The purpose of his study, Fitzmaurice explained, was "to call attention to the existence of this body of statements of principle [by the World Court], by extracting and assembling in classified form, and with such comment as may be necessary to explain their bearing and effect in the context in which they were made, all the conclusions and findings of the Court (and, within certain limits, of individual Judges) presenting features of general interest from the standpoint of international law and procedure." [9]

The problems with which the Tribunal has had to deal thus far may be classified into three broad categories: the legal and procedural problems of the Tribunal itself; the scope and limits of the managerial rights of the Secretary-General; and the rights and obligations of staff members.[10] The first category, it will be recalled, has already been explored in our discussion of the *modus operandi* of the Tribunal. Hence, attention will now be focused on the remaining two. In addition, the facts, laws, and consequences of the so-called political cases will be examined.

The Secretary-General, as noted, is the "chief administrative officer" of the United Nations under the Charter. As such, he is endowed with the supreme authority and responsibility in the administrative and personnel management of the Organization. This, however, should not blur the fact that the Secretary-General's functions and powers also take on a strongly political character.[11] Yet the framers of the Charter, Schwebel points out, intended to stress the primarily administrative nature of the Secretary-General's powers. The expression "chief administrative officer," he argues, "serves to emphasize the view of the authors of the Charter that, while the Secretary-General is to be more than the Organization's first functionary, he is also to be that functionary. Its stress of the Secretary-General's administrative responsibility tends to put his political authority in more subdued perspective." [12]

From the above mandate of the Charter, it follows that the Secretary-General must necessarily enjoy wide statutory and discretionary powers. However, these powers cannot be left unbridled, for the simple reason that unrestrained power is notoriously open to abuse. From its inception the Tribunal has been repeatedly called upon to define the scope and limits of the above powers. It declared at the outset:

> The United Nations Secretariat is a young organization which, since its establishment, has been almost continuously confronted with new problems of programmes demanding a high degree of flexibility and adaptability in deploying its resources . . . it is essential that broad powers be vested

in the Secretary-General to adapt the operations of the Secretariat to achieve the goals of efficient and economic operation and to meet the requirements of the standards of the Secretariat.

It continued:

The only effective limitation upon these powers in the present circumstances of the United Nations lies in the regulation of the manner of their exercise. It is also true that the exercise of broad powers without adequate procedural safeguards inevitably produces arbitrary limitation upon the exercise of any power. The maintenance of the authority of the Secretary-General to deal effectively and decisively with the work and operation of the Secretariat in conditions of flexibility and adaptability depends, in its exercise, in large measure upon the strict observance of procedural safeguards. In a very real sense the mode must be the measure of the power.[13]

Insofar as concerns the internal administration of the Organization, the Secretary-General has full discretionary powers. Thus the Tribunal declared in Judgment No. 2:

. . . it is not part of the functions of the Tribunal to express any view as to the administrative advantages of that change [a change in the methods of reporting proceedings] or as to the wisdom of particular measures proposed to effect it . . . .[14]

This point was repeatedly underlined in later judgments. In Judgment No. 17, the Tribunal said:

It is not the function of the Tribunal to deal with the internal administrative problems raised in the recommendations in the report of the Joint Appeals Board. Nor is it part of the function of the Tribunal to indicate views on alleged weaknesses in internal administrative procedures or actions taken under such procedure.[15]

Statements to the same effect are also found in Judgments 43–47, 49, and 75.[16] In the same vein, the Tribunal has ruled that "the determination of standards of qualification of the staff" lies solely with the Secretary-General and is therefore unreviewable by it.[17]

The Tribunal has further recognized the power of the Secretary-General to make any reductions in or abolition of posts. Such a power, it said, "may be necessary in order to observe due economy while providing adequately for the service of the United Nations."[18] The Tribunal has recognized the Secretary-General's authority, under the Staff Regulations, to terminate temporary-indefinite contracts; not to renew fixed-term contracts; to terminate permanent contracts; and to dismiss staff members for disciplinary reasons. At the same time, it has made clear the limits of the Secretary-General's powers. It has pointed out that the General Assembly "did not intend to give and did not give to the Secretary-General an absolutely discretionary power in respect of terminations." [19] It stressed that holders of temporary-indefinite contracts were entitled to certain rights and guarantees as members of the international civil service of the United Nations, "among the more essential of which are the right to appear before the Appeals Board and the right to be heard by this Tribunal." [20]

The discretionary powers of the Secretary-General in general and his power to terminate temporary-indefinite appointments in particular, the Tribunal said, "must be exercised *without improper motive* so that there shall be no misuse of power, since any such misuse of power would call for the rescinding of the decision." [21] It noted that, while Staff Regulation 9.1(c), which governs termination of temporary appointments,

. . . does not require the Secretary-General to state a specific reason or follow any particular procedure . . . this would not authorize an arbitrary or capricious exercise of the power of termination, nor the assignment of specious or untruthful reasons for the action taken, such as would connote a lack of good faith or due consideration for the rights of the staff member involved.[22]

Furthermore, the Secretary-General is required, in the words of the Tribunal, "to make a reasonably diligent and effective search for any vacant post to which the holder of an indeterminate contract whose post has been abolished can be assigned." [23]

In a separate opinion attached to Judgment No. 60, Jacob Mark Lashly, then a member of the Tribunal, reaffirmed that the General Assembly had clearly intended "to assign to the Secretary-General discretionary powers [in termination of temporary appointments] commensurate with the great responsibilities imposed upon him by virtue of his office and the duties assigned to it." He indicated that the Secretary-General's decision involving termination of temporary appointments could be declared illegal only when it was established that causal connection existed between such decision and irregularities or that motive of animosity or prejudice entered into or influenced his decision.[24]

More restricted is the power of the Secretary-General to terminate permanent appointments. This is inherent in the nature of such appointments. The Tribunal said:

This type of appointment [a permanent appointment] has been used from the inception of the Secretariat to ensure the stability of the international civil service and to create a genuine body of international civil servants freely selected by the Secretary-General. In accordance with the regulations established by the General Assembly, permanent appointments cannot be terminated except under staff regulations which enumerate precisely the reasons for and the conditions governing the termination of service.[25]

The Secretary-General, it went on, can act only under a provision of the Staff Regulations. Not only must he indicate the provision on which he proposes to rely, but he must conform with the conditions and procedures laid down in the Staff Regulations. If he fails to comply with these principles, the Tribunal declared, it is entitled to inquire whether the termination of employment is in accordance with the rules in force.[26]

In a case concerning termination of a permanent appointment for reasons of health, the Tribunal reaffirmed the rule that "permanent appointments can be terminated only upon a decision which has been reached by means of a complete, fair and reasonable procedure which must be carried out prior to such decision." Upon examination of the specific circumstances of the case, it found that "the Applicant has been denied due process in that a proper medical procedure was not followed by the Respondent." [27] As was the case with termination of temporary appointments, the Secretary-General is obligated to make a diligent search for another available post for the staff member concerned before terminating the latter's permanent appointment. The burden of proving that the Secretary-General made such a search, the Tribunal declared, rests on the Secretary-General.[28]

The Tribunal has construed the Secretary-General's power to dismiss the holder of a permanent appointment when the latter's "services . . . prove unsatisfactory." After examining both English and French texts of the provisions concerned, it concluded that the term "service" is applicable, not to the whole of the obligations incumbent upon staff members, but merely to their professional activities, i.e., "the carrying out of the tasks entrusted to them in the Secretariat." Thus the private, as distinguished from the professional, life of staff members was declared to be beyond the Secretary-General's control.[29]

The Tribunal has also stated that the Secretary-General's power, under Staff Regulation 10.2, to make summary dismissal for serious misconduct could be exercised "only when the proven misconduct obstructs the work or endangers the safety of the Secretariat organization or when acts of immorality are perpetrated in the course of official duties." The original purpose of the above provision, it stressed, was to enable the Secretary-General to "deal with acts obviously incompatible with continued membership of the staff." Only in those cases "where the misconduct is patent and where the interest of service requires immediate and final dismissal" can the exercise of the above power be justified, it said.[30]

In short, while the Secretary-General enjoys wide discretionary powers in matters relating to the internal administration of the Organization and may terminate staff members, regardless of the type of their contract, on the grounds specified in the Staff Regulations, his powers are subject to certain legal and procedural limitations. As Friedmann and Fatouros point out, he must, first, comply with the procedure set forth in the "integral law of the United Nations." [31] Second, he must make explicit and be prepared to justify when necessary, the reasons for his actions, in particular those involving terminations. Third, he must not be improperly motivated—that is, he must establish, when his decision is contested, that he acted neither from prejudice nor in bad faith.[32] To fail to do so is to invite the criticism of misuse of power —a ground on which the Tribunal can declare and has in fact declared the Secretary-General's actions and decisions illegal. Fourth, his decision must be based on a correct interpretation of a legal provision. Acting out of a mistake of law is thus another ground for the nullification of his decision.[33] Finally, the facts on which his decision is based must be correct.[34] The Tribunal, however, has generally refrained from pronouncing upon the validity of facts invoked by the Secretary-General when they relate to internal administrative practices.

As international civil servants, staff members of the United Nations have special duties and obligations as well as rights and privileges. The Tribunal thus recognized the duty of staff members to discharge their function and to regulate their conduct with the interests of only the United Nations in view, when it examined, in a series of disputes involving American staff members of the Secretariat, not only periodic reports on the latter's performance on the job, but their conduct outside the United Nations.[35] As already noted, the Tribunal has also recognized the power of the Secretary-General summarily to dismiss staff members when their misconduct is patently injurious to the interests of the Organization.

On the other hand, the Tribunal has expressed the hope that the so-called "principle of security of tenure" be preserved to the maximum possible extent. Reductions or abolition of posts, it said, should be effected

> . . . in such a manner which minimizes the sacrifices consequently inflicted upon individual officers and which preserves as far as may be possible in the circumstances the principle of security of tenure in accordance with the contracts applicable to individual cases.[36]

The above principle was inferentially reaffirmed when the Tribunal sustained a series of applications alleging, *inter alia*, that the Secretary-General's termination "violated the basic tenure rights of the applicant who held a permanent contract since it was not effected in accordance with the pertinent staff regulations." [37]

In Judgment No. 71, the Tribunal ruled that the applicant's business outside the Organization was incompatible with the obligation assumed by him as an international civil servant. Referring to the finding by a Review Board that "the whole history of the Applicant's business activities was 'marked by claims, debts and litigation,'" it declared:

> It is possible for an international civil servant, however honest his intentions, to be placed in a position either by poor judgment or bad luck, where his usefulness may be sufficiently impaired to justify termination of his service. The Applicant's situation is a case in point.[38]

An important statement on the nature of the legal tie between the Organization and its staff members was made in connection with an applicant's allegation that his acquired rights based on contract of employment could not be affected by unilateral alterations in the Staff Regulations and Rules. The Tribunal declared in a clear language that relations between staff members and the United Nations were not solely contractual in nature but also involved statutory elements. This, it said, was evidenced in the fact that Article 101 of the Charter gave the General Assembly the right unilaterally to establish and alter the legal regulations governing the staff, namely, the Staff Regulations.[39]

The Tribunal declared:

> In determining the legal position of staff members a distinction should be made between contractual elements and statutory elements:
>
> All matters being contractual which affect the personal status of each member—e.g., nature of his contract, salary, grade;
>
> All matters being statutory which affect in general the organization of the international civil service, and the need for its proper functioning—e.g., general rules that have no personal reference.
>
> While the contractual elements cannot be changed without the agreement of the two parties, the statutory elements on the other hand may always be changed at any time through regulations established by the General Assembly, and these changes are binding on staff members.[40]

Another way of explaining the above principle is that the legal position of the staff member is governed simultaneously by private and public laws. For, while contracts are of private law nature, statutory elements take on public law character. The latter are neither based on the express consent of those whom they govern nor can be changed by them. The practical advantage of distinguishing between contractual and statutory elements, however, is questioned by Friedmann and Fatouros. Describing the problem as "purely academic," they argue "even if the private law-contractual view is adopted, still, by virtue of clauses included in all contracts of employment of the UN Secretariat, certain matters would be governed by the Staff Regulations and Rules. Thus as the effects would be much the same in any case, the question of the legal status of the international civil servant is one of the choice of legal construction on a given factual basis." [41]

The right of staff members to receive salary, allowances, and benefits in exchange for and as a result of their service with the United Nations has frequently been the subject of the Tribunal's ruling. Generally, it has awarded arrears of salary when an application is adjudged well founded.[42] In other judgments where it found irregularity in the Secretary-General's actions relative to reclassification of staff members, the Tribunal ordered that the applicants be awarded the difference in salary after necessary adjustments have been made.[43] A basic principle applicable to all disputes concerning salary, allowances, and benefits appears to be that staff members enjoy these benefits only to the extent to which legal regulations expressly stipulate. Thus an interpretation of the Service Code of the ICAO has led the Tribunal to conclude that the Council of the Organization

. . . had the power to adopt another definition in 1960 by statutory action without the staff members who had a right to the previous system being entitled to continue to enjoy the benefits of that system after the entry into force of the amendment in question.[44]

When the Secretary-General opted for compensation in lieu of reinstatement with regard to a staff member whose termination had been declared illegal, the Tribunal ordered, *inter alia*, that the staff member be either "paid in every twelve months thereafter until her death such amount as she would normally have been entitled to expect as annual pension" or be paid the amount in lump sum.[45] On another occasion, the Tribunal was called upon to validate a staff member's prior service on the basis of the Pension Fund Regulations. Complex legal problems surrounding the case, however, caused the Tribunal to postpone its decision on merit pending communication to the Tribunal of further information by the parties.[46]

In connection with the right of home leave enjoyed by staff members, the decisions of the Administration bearing on the nationality and on the place of entitlement of staff members, respectively, have been contested. In the former case, a staff member possessing dual nationality sought unsuccessfully to rescind the decision of the Secretary-General to consider her as being of United States nationality for the purposes of the Staff Regulations and Rules. While recognizing the latter's right to home leave, the Tribunal found that her allegations were not tenable. Of home leave and other benefits enjoyed by staff members, the Tribunal said:

. . . every member as a consequence of his recruitment by the United Nations is entitled to the benefits provided for in the Staff Regulations and Rules. He enjoys those benefits in his own right and may file applications with the Tribunal alleging non–observance of his contract or conditions of employment, even if he is enjoying equivalent benefits indirectly as the spouse of another staff member.[47]

In the case concerning the place of entitlement, for purposes of home leave, of a staff member, the Tribunal examined the purpose of home leave as defined by a Committee of Experts on Salary, Allowances and Leave Systems. According to the Committee:

> . . . the purpose of home leave is to serve, in the first place, the interests of the Organization, i.e., to enable individual staff members to maintain their national ties and interests, and in particular their professional and official contacts, so that the "representative" character (in terms of different cultures and experience) of the staff as a whole is kept alive; and, in the second place, to afford the individual staff member the opportunity of renewing his personal ties and contacts and thereby to provide some measure of compensation for his "expatriated" status. Whilst the latter of the above two conditions should not be neglected, the Committee believes that in administering a home leave policy emphasis should be placed on the former.

The Committee went on to define "home" for leave purposes as:

> . . . the country of nationality provided the staff member has resided there within the ten-year period before appointment, or another country provided the staff member has resided there continuously for five years immediately preceding appointment.[48]

Applying these criteria to the facts of the case, the Tribunal found that the place of entitlement for the applicant had been erroneously determined and ordered rectification thereof.[49]

In brief, the Tribunal has gone a long way, not merely in clarifying the legal status of the international civil servant of the United Nations, but in delineating the boundaries of his duties, obligations, and privileges. In so doing it has given authoritative and binding interpretations of the Staff Regulations and Rules with regard to the conditions of service of the international civil service.

Because of the special position they occupy in the jurisprudence of the Tribunal, the so-called political cases, or the cases involving termination of American staff members of the Secretariat, to which references have been repeatedly made, deserve a somewhat detailed examination. It is therefore proposed to examine the facts of the cases, the decisions of the Tribunal, and their repercussions.

It is revealing to note that twenty-nine judgments,[50] or more than 32 percent of the judgments delivered thus far, are related, one way or another, to the now notorious McCarthy episode in the United States Senate. Twenty-one staff members are involved in these disputes.[51] Since the facts of these cases are broadly similar except for minor details, one typical case will be singled out for purposes of scrutiny, that of Joel Gordon, Judgment No. 29.

Gordon entered the service of the United Nations in 1946 as an economic affairs officer in the Department of Economic Affairs. After holding a temporary contract, he received a permanent contract in 1947. In the early part of October, 1952, he appeared as a witness before both a Federal Grand Jury and the Internal Security Subcommittee of the United States Senate which was investigating the activities of United States citizens employed by the United Nations. At the Senate hearing Gordon refused to answer some of the questions put to him, invoking the privilege under the Fifth Amendment to the United States Constitution.[52] The questions concerned: whether he had ever been a member of the Communist Party; whether he was not engaged in any subversive activities against the United States Government; and whether he had ever engaged in espionage.[53]

On October 22, 1952 he was informed in writing by Secretary-General Lie that the latter had decided to suspend him "immediately with pay, pending my investigation of this entire matter." The Secretary-General specifically referred to his refusal to answer questions in the Senate hearing. On December 1, 1952 the Secretary-General sent him the "opinion of the Commission of Jurists," drawing his attention to "the fourth Part of this report which relates to 'Principles with Regard to Officers Accused or Suspected of Disloyalty to the Host Country.'" The Secretary-General later indicated his decision to accept the Commission's recommendation. He warned that unless Gordon notified the appropriate United States authorities of his intention to withdraw the plea of privilege and to answer the questions put to him, he would be compelled to terminate his employment in the United Nations.[54]

Gordon replied on December 4, 1952 that he could not agree with the opinion of the Commission of Jurists and asked the Secretary-General to reconsider his decision. On receiving this reply, the Secretary-General informed Gordon on December 5, 1952 that his attitude constituted a "fundamental breach of the obligations laid down in Staff Regulation 1.4" and that, consequently, his employment in the secretariat had been terminated. This led Gordon to apply, with the Secretary-General's consent, directly to the Tribunal on February 17, 1953 for reinstatement in his former post, arrears of salary, and damages. Later he substituted for his request for reinstatement a claim for further damages amounting to five years' salary.[55]

In support of his application, Gordon argued:

1. That the decision contested was illegal and void, as it resulted from improper pressure exercised upon the Secretary-General by an agency of a Member State, i.e., the Internal Security Subcommittee of the Judiciary Committee of the United States Senate;

2. That the termination of his employment was improper in that it was based on arbitrary and extraneous political considerations;

3. That the termination violated the basic tenure rights to which he was entitled as a holder of a permanent contract since it was not effected in accordance with the pertinent staff regulations;

4. That the invocation of the privilege under the Fifth Amendment did not constitute a breach of the Staff Regulations, particularly of article 1.4, since under American law the exercise of the privilege did not create an inference of guilt;

5. That the Secretary-General violated principles of due process in placing him upon special leave and in failing to make the consultations with the joint bodies prescribed in staff regulations 8.1 and 8.2 dealing with staff relations.[56]

The Secretary-General answered these charges by denying that his decision resulted either from pressure or improper motivation. He pointed out in particular that Gordon was duty bound, under the Charter and Staff Regulations 1.4 "to conduct himself at all times in a manner befitting his status as an international civil servant and to remain worthy of trust and confidence." He further argued that the refusal to answer by claiming the constitutional privilege, while legal under American law, gave rise to the inference that Gordon was or had been engaged in activities directed towards the violent overthrow of the government of a member state. For these reasons, the Secretary-General asserted, Gordon was guilty of serious misconduct and his services were shown to be unsatisfactory, thus justifying termination under the terms of Staff Regulations 9.1(a) and 10.2. Finally, the Secretary-General refuted the charge of denial of due process by pointing out (1) that Gordon was given an opportunity to revoke his decision and (2) that a group of senior Secretariat officials were consulted before the Secretary-General took the final step.[57]

In a judgment pronounced on August 21, 1953, the Tribunal

first dealt with the nature of permanent appointment. Such an appointment, it said, had been used from the inception of the Secretariat to ensure the stability of the international civil service and to enhance the stature of the international civil servants of the United Nations. Accordingly, the Secretary-General had a special duty to respect the stability of permanent appointment and to terminate it only under a provision of the Staff Regulations. It said that the Secretary-General must make explicit the provision upon which he proposed to rely and must conform with the procedure stipulated in the Staff Regulations.[58]

After emphasizing that the applicant had held a permanent contract and that his professional ability and devotion had not been disputed, the Tribunal turned to the report of the commission of three jurists which the Secretary-General had consulted. The jurists had argued in their report that the refusal to answer the questions constituted a fundamental breach of the obligations laid down in Staff Regulation 1.4. [59] It was their opinion that because of the contractual relationship between a staff member and the Secretary-General, the latter had the right, in the case of a fundamental breach by a staff member of his obligations under the Staff Regulations, to terminate appointments without indemnity, even if the Staff Regulations did not specifically refer to such a right.[60]

The above opinion, the Tribunal noted, disregarded the nature of permanent contracts, described at the outset, as well as the character of regulations governing termination of employment laid down by the General Assembly under Article 101 of the Charter. It pointed out, however, that the Secretary-General neither fully complied with recommendations of the jurists nor advanced their arguments before the Tribunal. Instead, he awarded an indemnity to the applicant and held, before the Tribunal, that the breach of Staff Regulation 1.4 could be treated as both unsatisfactory service and serious misconduct enabling the Secretary-General to dismiss the Applicant without imposing disciplinary measures. It was for the Tribunal therefore to inquire whether the above argument was valid within the meaning of Staff Regulations 9.1 (termination of employment for unsatisfactory services) and 10 (summary dismissal for serious misconduct).[61]

With respect to the former, the Tribunal pointed out that the term "services" as used in the Staff Regulations and Rules referred solely to professional behavior within the United Nations and did not cover all the obligation incumbent upon a staff member. It observed:

If it is admitted that the invoking of a constitutional privilege in respect of acts outside a staff member's professional duties constitutes a breach of article 1.4 of the Staff Regulations, this fact cannot be considered as unsatisfactory services and cannot fall within the purview of article 9.1.

On the other hand, the Tribunal continued, misconduct punishable under Article 10 could be construed more broadly: it could be either misconduct committed in the exercise of a staff member's professional duties or acts committed outside his professional activities but prohibited by provisions creating general obligations for staff members.[62]

The Tribunal then considered whether the allegations made against the applicant constituted serious misconduct justifying his summary dismissal by the Secretary-General without reference to the Joint Disciplinary Committee. It took note of the fact that the provision concerning summary dismissal for serious misconduct had been introduced by the General Assembly to cope with only exceptional cases—"cases where the misconduct is patent and where the interest of the service requires immediate and final separation." The applicant's recourse to the privilege provided in the constitution of his country, the Tribunal declared, fell short of "serious misconduct" within the above meaning, which alone under article 10.2 of the Staff Regulations and pertinent Rules justified the Secretary-General in dismissing a staff member summarily without the safeguard afforded by the disciplinary procedure.[63]

The Tribunal therefore declared the Secretary-General's decision to terminate the applicant's employment illegal and awarded (1) "Full salary up to the date of this judgment less the amount paid at termination in lieu of notice and less also the amount of termination indemnity," (2) compensation in the amount of $6,000 in lieu of reinstatement, and (3) legal costs in the amount of $300. [64]

In other cases where the applicants requested the rescission of the decision contested, i.e., reinstatement, rather than compensation in lieu thereof, the Tribunal so ordered. Nine applications involving temporary contracts, however, were rejected on the grounds that the Tribunal was not competent to review the Secretary-General's decision which had been taken, in conformity with Staff

Regulation 9.1(c), in what he regarded as the interest of the United Nations, and, furthermore that no proof had been submitted to establish improper motivation on the part of the Secretary-General.[65]

Where the Tribunal ordered the rescinding of termination, the Secretary-General without exception took advantage of the option granted to him under Article 9, paragraph 1, of the Statute, of paying compensation in lieu of reinstatement. A grave crisis soon developed, however, when the General Assembly refused to appropriate funds necessary for implementing the Tribunal's judgments. This eventually led the General Assembly to request an advisory opinion from the International Court of Justice. In a resolution passed on December 9, 1953 the General Assembly decided to submit the following questions to the International Court of Justice for an advisory opinion:

(1) Having regard to the Statute of the United Nations Administrative Tribunal and to any other relevant instruments and to the relevant records, has the General Assembly the right on any grounds to refuse to give effect to an award of compensation made by that Tribunal in favour of a staff member of the United Nations whose contract of service has been terminated without his assent?

(2) If the answer given by the Court to the question (1) is in the affirmative, what are the principal grounds upon which the General Assembly could lawfully exercise such a right? [66]

The Court examined all relevant documents and written statements from the I.L.O. and the governments of France, the United Kingdom, the United States, the Philippines, Mexico, Chile, Iraq, China, Guatemala, Turkey, and Ecuador, and also heard oral statements from a number of eminent jurists representing the Secretary-General and the governments of the United States, France, Greece, the United Kingdom, and the Netherlands, respectively. In an advisory opinion delivered on July 13, 1954, it first established the indisputably judicial character of the Tribunal. An examination of all the pertinent provisions in the Statute of the Tribunal left no doubt to the Court that the Tribunal was neither a subordinate organ of the General Assembly nor a mere advisory body, but "an independent and truly judicial body pronouncing final judgments without appeal within the limited field of its functions." [67]

According to a well-established and generally recognized principle of law, the Court noted, a judgment rendered by such a judicial body was *res judicata* and had binding force between the parties to the dispute. The Court therefore proceeded to determine who were to be regarded as parties bound by an award of compensation made in favor of a staff member of the United Nations whose contract of service had been terminated without his assent. It held that because such a contract of service was concluded between the staff member concerned and the Secretary-General in his capacity as the chief administrative officer of the United Nations Organization, acting on behalf of that Organization as its legal representative, the parties to a dispute concerning termination of such a contract before the Tribunal were *the staff member concerned* and *the United Nations Organization, represented by the Secretary-General.* These parties, it added, would become bound by the judgment of the Tribunal.[68] The Court declared:

This judgment is, according to Article 10 of the Tribunal's Statute, final and without appeal. The Statute has provided for no kind of review. As this final judgment has binding force on the United Nations Organization as the juridical person responsible for the proper observance of the contract of service, that Organization becomes legally bound to carry out the judgment and to pay the compensation awarded to the staff member. It follows that the General Assembly, as an organ of the United Nations, must likewise be bound by the judgment.[69]

The Court next treated the question whether the General Assembly would in certain exceptional circumstances be legally entitled to refuse to give effect to awards of compensation made by the Tribunal. Underlining the judicial character of the Tribunal, noted above, it expressed the view that, in order that the judgments pronounced by such a judicial tribunal could be subjected to review to any body other than the Tribunal itself, it would be necessary that the statute of that tribunal or some other legal instrument governing it should contain an express provision to that effect. While the General Assembly had the power to amend the Statute of the Tribunal by virtue of Article 2 of that Statute and to provide for means of redress by another organ, the Court noted, it had not exercised that power. Hence there was no legal ground upon which it could proceed to review judgments already pronounced by the Tribunal, the Court said.[70]

In the remainder of the advisory opinion the Court examined and refuted the principal contentions which had been put forward by the various governments; these were (1) that the General

Assembly lacked the legal power to establish a tribunal competent to render judgments binding on the United Nations; (2) that even if it had an implied power, that did not enable the General Assembly to establish a tribunal with authority to make decisions binding on the General Assembly itself; and (3) that the Court should follow the precedent set by the League in 1946 when its Assembly rejected certain awards of its Administrative Tribunal. We shall take note of a few important points made by the Court in the course of the refutation, rather than examine the details of the Court's juridical reasoning in refuting the above arguments.

On the *raison d'etre* and legality of the Tribunal, the Court commented:

> When the Secretariat was organized, a situation arose in which the relations between the staff members and the Organization were governed by a complex code of law. This code consisted of the Staff Regulations established by the General Assembly, defining the fundamental rights and obligations of the staff, and the Staff Rules, made by the Secretary-General in order to implement the Staff Regulations. It was inevitable that there would be disputes between the Organization and staff members as to their rights and duties. The Charter contains no provision which authorizes any of the principal organs of the United Nations to adjudicate upon these disputes, and Article 105 secures for the United Nations jurisdictional immunities in national courts. It would, in the opinion of the Court, hardly be consistent with the expressed aim of the Charter to promote freedom and justice for individuals and with the constant preoccupation of the United Nations Organization to promote this aim that it should afford no judicial or arbitral remedy to its own staff for the settlement of any disputes which may arise between it and them.[71]

In short, the Court said, the power to establish a tribunal arose "by necessary intendment out of the Charter." The Charter, furthermore, clearly intended that the General Assembly should be the agency by which such a power might be exercised. For, according to the Court, the Charter gave the General Assembly authority, not only to "establish such subsidiary organs as it deems necessary for the performance of its functions" (Art. 22), but also to regulate staff relations (Art. 101, par. 1).[72]

The Court also observed that the assignment of the budgetary function to the General Assembly could not be regarded as conferring upon it the right to refuse to give effect to obligations already incurred by the Organization, to which category belonged the obligations arising out of an award of the Tribunal.[73] As to the argument that because the Tribunal was a subsidiary, subordinate, or secondary organ, its judgments could not bind the General Assembly which had established it, the Court remarked:

By establishing the Administrative Tribunal, the General Assembly was not delegating the performance of its own functions: it was exercising a power which it had under the Charter to regulate staff relations. In regard to the Secretariat, the General Assembly is given by the Charter a power to make regulations, but not a power to adjudicate upon, or otherwise deal with, particular instances.

It went on to say:

There can be no doubt that the Administrative Tribunal is subordinate in the sense that the General Assembly can abolish the Tribunal by repealing the Statute, that it can amend the Statute or provide for review of the future decisions of the Tribunal and that it can amend the Staff Regulations and make new ones. . . . But the contention that the General Assembly is inherently incapable of creating a tribunal competent to make decisions binding on itself cannot be accepted. It cannot be justified by analogy to national laws, for it is common practice in national legislatures to create courts with the capacity to render decisions legally binding on the legislatures which brought them into being.[74]

The argument invoking the "precedent" of the League was dismissed by pointing out "the complete lack of identity between the two situations." [75]

The above opinion of the Court was reached by nine votes to three. The three dissenting members of the Court were Judges A. Alvarez, G. H. Hackworth, and Levi Carneiro. Judge B. Winiarski, while voting in favor of the opinion, chose to append a statement of his separate opinion. Judge Hackworth, an American member on the international bench, in disagreeing with the majority opinion, argued that the General Assembly was not bound to effectuate a decision "which is not juridically sound, and which, because of the absence of the juridical plausibility, does not command the respect of the Assembly." [76]

He asserted that the General Assembly had a right to review a decision of the Tribunal, as a corollary to its duty to consider and approve the budget of the Organization and to maintain a high standard of efficiency and integrity. The General Assembly, in his opinion, might lawfully exercise that right with respect to any decision which did not commend itself to respectful and favorable considerations. Thus, he argued, the principal grounds upon which the General Assembly might lawfully exercise a right to decline to give effect to an award were: (1) that the award is *ultra vires*; (2) that the award reveals manifest defects or deficiency in the administration of justice; (3) that the award does not reflect a faithful application of the Charter, the Statute of the Tribunal, or the Staff Rules and Regulations, to the facts of the case; and (4) that the amount of the award is obviously either excessive or inadequate.[77]

In brief, not only did the Court firmly establish the judicial character of the Tribunal, but it considerably enhanced the authority and respectability of its judgment. This was a significant contribution to the continued existence as well as the progressive development of the Tribunal. Moreover, the Court's advisory opinion gave a direct impetus to the 1955 amendment to the statute introducing a procedure for review of the Tribunal's judgment. The details regarding the procedure have already been examined.

CHAPTER 6

CONCLUSIONS

IT IS CLEAR that the Tribunal fills one of the important needs of international administration. Its obvious function is to delineate the demarcation line between the discretionary and statutory powers of the Secretary-General on the one hand, and the legal and contractual rights of staff members of the United Nations on the other. Its latent function is not merely to protect staff rights but to enhance the dignity and authority of the Secretary-General's administrative actions and decisions. Evidently, this is not only a necessary, but an indispensable, role for the personnel administration of the United Nations.

On the other hand, certain limitations are clearly visible in the work of the Tribunal. For one thing, it has no competence over disputes involving disciplinary measures except those which result in summary dismissal. In view of the purely advisory nature of the decisions of the Joint Appeals Board, which has competence over disciplinary cases, and of the possibility that disciplinary measures short of dismissal are perfectly capable of causing injustice to the staff member concerned, this may very well be regarded as a gap in the legal protection of staff rights.

Far more serious, however, is the limitation inherent in the types of remedies the Tribunal is competent to award. In theory it can choose from among (1) rescission of the decision contested, (2) performance of the specific obligation invoked, and (3) payment of compensation in lieu of rescission and performance; in reality the power to make such a choice exists in name only. The Secretary-General invariably invokes the privilege, granted to him by the Statute, to choose the third alternative. This must be considered as a serious deficiency in law. That monetary compensation can never be a satisfactory substitute for reinstatement in termination cases is intuitively obvious. The rationale behind the optional clause, i.e., that the interests of the Organization must remain unimpaired at all costs, is both understandable and justified; on the other hand, the practical effect of that rationale as manifested over the past fourteen years, i.e., the penalization of staff members at all times, however justified their complaints and however outrageous the injuries inflicted upon them by unwarranted actions and decisions of the Secretary-General, is difficult, if not impossible, to justify.

A feasible solution would appear to be to amend the Statute so as to empower the Tribunal to rule, in exceptional cases, that the optional clause will not apply to the judgment concerned. The optional clause, meanwhile, would continue to be applicable to other cases. The Tribunal would have to resort to the above course of action only when and if it were fully convinced that a grave injustice would be done by not reinstating the staff member concerned. It must, of course, carefully weigh the injury that would be suffered by the staff member concerned against the probable effects on the operating effectiveness of reinstatement. The significant value of such an amendment would be, not merely that it would be overtly resorted to, but that it would force the Secretary-General to be more cautious in exercising his power to terminate staff members. The goal, in other words, is to do preventive, rather than merely remedial, justice.

The amendment might conceivably serve to promote the feeling of security among staff members and thereby to enhance the general prestige of the international civil service. Another likely effect of the amendment is the increase in the volume of the Tribunal's judicial business. If staff members were persuaded that the Tribunal was capable of substantive, as opposed to purely monetary, justice, they might make more use of it. This might eventually call for the operation of the Tribunal on a permanent basis with full-time members. It may be observed in this connection that in determining the qualifications of its members a balanced emphasis is necessary—that is, administrative experience and training should be considered on a par with experience and competence in legal matters. In the past only lip service has been paid to this principle.

The judgments of the Tribunal provide some evidence that the *career* international civil servant, i.e., the holder of a permanent appointment, enjoys a substantial measure of employment security in the United Nations. If one may generalize from the Tribunal's record thus far, then it may be said that the career man has substantially less chance of being dismissed than the temporary employee. Furthermore, when dismissed, the career man may appeal to the Tribunal with the expectation that he will be more likely to win the dispute than to lose it. The contrary is true of the temporary employee. Winning the dispute, it should be noted, is not identical with winning his job back, however. The latter, unfortunately for the staff member, lies in the realm of impossibility under the Statute now in force.

As already noted, in the final analysis, the Tribunal is clearly conducive to the good administration of the Organization. As long as the Organization is staffed by human beings rather than by supermen or robots, there will continue to be employment disputes. The Secretary-General will continue to make decisions, justified or unjustified, legal or illegal, affecting the personal contractual status of staff members who, naturally, will continue to make complaints. In short, the need for a judicial organ, marked as it must be by the impartiality, justice, authority, and effectiveness of its judgments, is perennially present. The Tribunal, by filling that need, performs a patently useful service to the Organization.

The precise nature of the contribution which the Tribunal makes to the maintenance of staff morale is difficult to measure. Equally unfathomable is its probable utility as a psychological deterrent of the Secretary-General's arbitrary action. That both the staff and the Secretary-General continue to believe in the value of the Tribunal and thus favor its continued existence, however, is evident from the positions they have taken in connection with the revision of the Statute on several occasions. The Tribunal appears to demonstrate that administration and law are mutually complementary, and not mutually exclusive or antithetical. Administrative power must be kept in proper limits by law. Law, on the other hand, is not an end in itself, but only a means to an end. Its objective, in the ultimate analysis, is no different from that of administration—to ensure the maximum practicable justice and happiness for the community of men. The experience of the Tribunal suggests that an interplay between law and administration can be a mutually beneficial one.

The Tribunal has made an important contribution to the development of the law of employment relations and of what may eventually become international administrative law. It has effectively illustrated legal and procedural problems involved in the above process. Furthermore, it may be argued that the Tribunal has marked another important, if small, step toward improving the *locus standi* of individuals before international tribunals. Although the Tribunal's is a highly limited and specialized competence, the fact remains that it is an *international* tribunal—a tribunal which is open to staff members of all nationalities and which deals with disputes arising between them and the United Nations Organization. Hence, the experience gained by the Tribunal can provide a useful guide to the gradual extension of the competence of the International Court of Justice to both individuals and international organizations. In a small but nonetheless real sense, the Tribunal helps to bring the world a step closer to that everlasting ideal—the rule of law, and not of men.

Just as the problems with which the international civil service must grapple will multiply with its steady growth, so will the role of the Tribunal in the definition, clarification, and protection of the international civil servant visibly expand. More than ever before, the Tribunal will be called upon to fulfill the difficult but essential function—that of maintaining an equilibrium between the interests of the Organization and those of individual staff members, between the needs of the whole and those of its component parts. The two need not always compete; they can and must coexist.

APPENDIX 1

STATUTE OF THE ADMINISTRATIVE TRIBUNAL
OF THE UNITED NATIONS

as adopted by the General Assembly by resolution 351 A (IV) on 24 November 1949 and amended by resolution 782 B (VIII) on 9 December 1953 and by resolution 957 (X) on 8 November 1955

ARTICLE 1

A Tribunal is established by the present Statute to be known as the United Nations Administrative Tribunal.

ARTICLE 2

1 The Tribunal shall be competent to hear and pass judgement upon applications alleging non-observance of contracts of employment of staff members of the Secretariat of the United Nations or of the terms of appointment of such staff members. The words "contracts" and "terms of appointment" include all pertinent regulations and rules in force at the time of alleged non-observance, including the staff pension regulations.

2 The Tribunal shall be open:

(a) To any staff member of the Secretariat of the United Nations even after his employment has ceased, and to any person who has succeeded to the staff member's rights on his death;

(b) To any other person who can show that he is entitled to rights under any contract or terms of appointment, including the provisions of staff regulations and rules upon which the staff member could have relied.

3 In the event of a dispute as to whether the Tribunal has competence, the matter shall be settled by the decision of the Tribunal.

4 The Tribunal shall not be competent, however, to deal with any applications where the cause of complaint arose prior to 1 January 1950.

ARTICLE 3

1 The Tribunal shall be composed of seven members, no two of whom may be nationals of the same State. Only three shall sit in any particular case.

2 The members shall be appointed by the General Assembly for three years, and they may be re-appointed; provided, however, that of the members initially appointed, the terms of two members shall expire at the end of one year and the terms of two members shall expire at the end of two years. A member appointed to replace a member whose term of office has not expired shall hold office for the remainder of his predecessor's term.

3 The Tribunal shall elect its President and its two Vice-Presidents from among its members.

4 The Secretary-General shall provide the Tribunal with an Executive Secretary and such other staff as may be considered necessary.

5 No member of the Tribunal can be dismissed by the General Assembly unless the other members are of the unanimous opinion that he is unsuited for further service.

6 In case of a resignation of a member of the Tribunal, the resignation shall be addressed to the President of the Tribunal for transmission to the Secretary-General. This last notification makes the place vacant.

ARTICLE 4

The Tribunal shall hold ordinary sessions at dates to be fixed by its rules, subject to there being cases on its list which, in the opinion of the President, justify holding the session. Extraordinary sessions may be convoked by the President when required by the cases on the list.

ARTICLE 5

1 The Secretary-General of the United Nations shall make the administrative arrangements necessary for the functioning of the Tribunal.

2 The expenses of the Tribunal shall be borne by the United Nations.

ARTICLE 6

1 Subject to the provisions of the present Statute, the Tribunal shall establish its rules.

2 The rules shall include provisions concerning:

(a) Election of the President and Vice-Presidents;

(b) Composition of the Tribunal for its sessions;

(c) Presentation of applications and the procedure to be followed in respect to them;

(d) Intervention by persons to whom the Tribunal is open under paragraph 2 of article 2, whose rights may be affected by the judgement;

(e) Hearing, for purposes of information, of persons to whom the Tribunal is open under paragraph 2 of article 2, even though they are not parties to the case; and generally

(f) Other matters relating to the functioning of the Tribunal.

ARTICLE 7

1 An application shall not be receivable unless the person concerned has previously submitted the dispute to the joint appeals body provided for in the staff regulations and the latter has communicated its opinion to the Secretary-General, except where the Secretary-General and the applicant have agreed to submit the application directly to the Administrative Tribunal.

2 In the event of the joint body's recommendations being favourable to the application submitted to it, and in so far as this is the case, an application to the Tribunal shall be receivable if the Secretary-General has:

(a) Rejected the recommendations;
(b) Failed to take any action within the thirty days following the communication of the opinion; or
(c) Failed to carry out the recommendations within the thirty days following the communication of the opinion.

3 In the event that the recommendations made by the joint body and accepted by the Secretary-General are unfavourable to the applicant, and in so far as this is the case, the application shall be receivable, unless the joint body unanimously considers that it is frivolous.

4 An application shall not be receivable unless it is filed within ninety days reckoned from the respective dates and periods referred to in paragraph 2 above, or within ninety days reckoned from the date of the communication of the joint body's opinion containing recommendations unfavourable to the applicant. If the circumstance rendering the application receivable by the Tribunal, pursuant to paragraphs 2 and 3 above, is anterior to the date of announcement of the first session of the Tribunal, the time limit of ninety days shall begin to run from that date. Nevertheless, the said time limit on his behalf shall be extended to one year if the heirs of a deceased staff member or the trustee of a staff member who is not in a position to manage his own affairs, file the application in the name of the said staff member.

5 In any particular case the Tribunal may decide to suspend the provisions regarding time limits.

6 The filing of an application shall not have the effect of suspending the execution of the decision contested.

7 Applications may be filed in any of the five official languages of the United Nations.

ARTICLE 8

The oral proceedings of the Tribunal shall be held in public unless the Tribunal decides that exceptional circumstances require that they be held in private.

ARTICLE 9

1 If the Tribunal finds that the application is well founded, it shall order the rescinding of the decision contested or the specific performance of the

obligation invoked. At the same time the Tribunal shall fix the amount of compensation to be paid to the applicant for the injury sustained should the Secretary-General, within thirty days of the notification of the judgement, decide, in the interest of the United Nations, that the applicant shall be compensated without further action being taken in his case; provided that such compensation shall not exceed the equivalent of two years' net base salary of the applicant. The Tribunal may, however, in exceptional cases, when it considers it justified, order the payment of a higher indemnity. A statement of the reasons for the Tribunal's decision shall accompany each such order.

2 Should the Tribunal find that the procedure prescribed in the Staff Regulations or Staff Rules has not been observed, it may, at the request of the Secretary-General and prior to the determination of the merits, order the case remanded for institution or correction of the required procedure. Where a case is remanded, the Tribunal may order the payment of compensation, not to exceed the equivalent of three months' net base salary, to the applicant for such loss as may have been caused by the procedural delay.

3 In all applicable cases, compensation shall be fixed by the Tribunal and paid by the United Nations or, as appropriate, by the specialized agency participating under article 14.

ARTICLE 10

1 The Tribunal shall take all decisions by a majority vote.

2 Subject to the provisions of articles 11 and 12, the judgements of the Tribunal shall be final and without appeal.

3 The judgements shall state the reasons on which they are based.

4 The judgements shall be drawn up, in any of the five official languages of the United Nations, in two originals, which shall be deposited in the archives of the Secretariat of the United Nations.

5 A copy of the judgement shall be communicated to each of the parties in the case. Copies shall also be made available on request to interested persons.

ARTICLE 11

1 If a Member State, the Secretary-General or the person in respect of whom a judgement has been rendered by the Tribunal (including any one who has succeeded to that person's rights on his death) objects to the judgement on the ground that the Tribunal has exceeded its jurisdiction or competence or that the Tribunal has failed to exercise jurisdiction vested in it, or has erred on a question of law relating to the provisions of the Charter of the United Nations, or has committed a fundamental error in procedure which has occasioned a failure of justice, such Member State, the Secretary-General or the person concerned may, within thirty days from the date of the judgement, make a written application to the Committee established by paragraph 4 of this article asking the Committee to

request an advisory opinion of the International Court of Justice on the matter.

2 Within thirty days from the receipt of an application under paragraph 1 of this article, the Committee shall decide whether or not there is a substantial basis for the application. If the Committee decides that such a basis exists, it shall request an advisory opinion of the Court, and the Secretary-General shall arrange to transmit to the Court the views of the person referred to in paragraph 1.

3 If no application is made under paragraph 1 of this article, or if a decision to request an advisory opinion has not been taken by the Committee, within the periods prescribed in this article, the judgement of the Tribunal shall become final. In any case in which a request has been made for an advisory opinion, the Secretary-General shall either give effect to the opinion of the Court or request the Tribunal to convene specially in order that it shall confirm its original judgement, or give a new judgement, in conformity with the opinion of the Court. If not requested to convene specially the Tribunal shall at its next session confirm its judgement or bring it into conformity with the opinion of the Court.

4 For the purpose of this article, a Committee is established and authorized under paragraph 2 of Article 96 of the Charter to request advisory opinions of the Court. The Committee shall be composed of the Member States the representatives of which have served on the General Committee of the most recent regular session of the General Assembly. The Committee shall meet at United Nations Headquarters and shall establish its own rules.

5 In any case in which award of compensation has been made by the Tribunal in favour of the person concerned and the Committee has requested an advisory opinion under paragraph 2 of this article, the Secretary-General, if satisfied that such person will otherwise be handicapped in protecting his interests, shall within fifteen days of the decision to request an advisory opinion make an advance payment to him of one-third of the total amount of compensation awarded by the Tribunal less such termination benefits, if any, as have already been paid. Such advance payment shall be made on condition that, within thirty days of the action of the Tribunal under paragraph 3 of this article, such person shall pay back to the United Nations the amount, if any, by which the advance payment exceeds any sum to which he is entitled in accordance with the opinion of the Court.

ARTICLE 12

The Secretary-General or the applicant may apply to the Tribunal for a revision of a judgement on the basis of the discovery of some fact of such a nature as to be a decisive factor, which fact was, when the judgement was given, unknown to the Tribunal and also to the party claiming revision, always provided that such ignorance was not due to negligence. The application must be made within thirty days of the discovery of the fact and within one year of the date of the judgement. Clerical or arithmetical mistakes in judgements, or errors arising therein from any accidental slip or omission, may at any time be corrected by the Tribunal either of its own motion or on the application of any of the parties.

ARTICLE 13

The present Statute may be amended by decisions of the General Assembly.

ARTICLE 14

The competence of the Tribunal may be extended to any specialized agency brought into relationship with the United Nations in accordance with the provisions of Articles 57 and 63 of the Charter upon the terms established by a special agreement to be made with each such agency by the Secretary-General of the United Nations. Each such special agreement shall provide that the agency concerned shall be bound by the judgements of the Tribunal and be responsible for the payment of any compensation awarded by the Tribunal in respect of a staff member of that agency and shall include, *inter alia*, provisions concerning the agency's participation in the administrative arrangements for the functioning of the Tribunal and concerning its sharing the expenses of the Tribunal.

APPENDIX 2

RULES OF THE ADMINISTRATIVE TRIBUNAL
OF THE UNITED NATIONS
*as adopted by the Tribunal on 7 June 1950 and amended on 20 December
1951, 9 December 1954, 30 November 1955, 4 December 1958 and 14
September 1962.*[1]

Chapter I. Organization
ARTICLE 1
Subject to any contrary decision of the General Assembly of the United
Nations, the term of office of members of the Tribunal shall commence on
the first day of January in the year following their appointment by the
General Assembly.

ARTICLE 2
1 At its plenary session each year, the Tribunal shall elect a President,
a first Vice-President and a second Vice-President for one year. The President
and Vice-Presidents thus elected shall take up their duties forthwith.
They may be re-elected.

2 The retiring President and Vice-Presidents shall remain in office until
their successors are elected.

3 If the President (or a Vice-President) should cease to be a member
of the Tribunal or should resign the office of President (or Vice-President)
before the expiration of his normal term, an election shall be held for the
purpose of appointing a successor for the unexpired portion of the term.
In the case of a vacancy of a Vice-President, the President may arrange
for the election of a successor by correspondence.

4 The elections shall be made by a majority vote.

---

1 A/CN.5/1, AT/7, AT/9, AT/10, AT/12 and AT/13.

ARTICLE 3

1 The President shall direct the work of the Tribunal and of its secretariat; he shall represent the Tribunal in all administrative matters; he shall preside at the meetings of the Tribunal.

2 If the President is unable to act, he shall designate one of the Vice-Presidents to act as President. In the absence of any such designation by the President, the first Vice-President or, in the event of the latter's incapacity, the second Vice-President shall act as President.

3 No case shall be heard by the Tribunal except under the chairmanship of the President or one of the Vice-Presidents.

ARTICLE 4

1 The Tribunal shall have an Executive Secretary and other staff placed at its disposal by the Secretary-General of the United Nations.

2 The Executive Secretary, if unable to act, shall be replaced by an official appointed by the Secretary-General.

Chapter II. Sessions

ARTICLE 5

1 The Tribunal shall hold a plenary session once a year (normally during the last quarter of the year), for the purpose of election of officers and any other matters affecting the administration or operation of the Tribunal. When, however, there are no cases on the list which in the opinion of the President would justify the holding of a session for their consideration, the President may, after consulting the other members of the Tribunal, decide to postpone the plenary session to a later date.

2 A special plenary session may be convened by the President when, in his opinion, it is necessary to deal with a question affecting the administration or operation of the Tribunal. Notice of the convening of a special plenary session shall be given to the members of the Tribunal at least thirty days in advance of the date of the opening of such a session.

3 Four members of the Tribunal shall constitute a quorum for plenary sessions.

4 The plenary sessions of the Tribunal shall be held at the Headquarters of the United Nations, except that the President may, if circumstances require, fix a different place after consultation with the Executive Secretary.

ARTICLE 6

1 The President shall designate the three members of the Tribunal who, in accordance with article 3 of the Statute, shall constitute the Tribunal for the purpose of sitting in each particular case or group of cases. The President may, in addition, designate one or more members of the Tribunal to serve as alternates.

2 In conformity with article 4 of the Statute, the Tribunal shall hold ordinary sessions for the purpose of considering cases. An ordinary session of the Tribunal shall be held each year during the period of the plenary session and in the second quarter of the year. Ordinary sessions shall only be held subject to there being cases on the list which by their number or

urgency justify, in the opinion of the President, the holding of the session. The decision of the President with respect to the opening of the ordinary sessions shall be communicated to the members of the Tribunal at least thirty days before the convening thereof.

3 Extraordinary sessions for the consideration of cases may be convened by the President when, in his opinion, the number or urgency of the cases on the list requires such sessions. Notice of the convening of an extraordinary session shall be given to the members of the Tribunal at least fifteen days in advance of the date of the opening of such sessions.

4 Ordinary and extraordinary sessions of the Tribunal shall be convened at dates and places to be set by the President after consultation with the Executive Secretary.

5 The Executive Secretary shall send to the members of the Tribunal, designated by the President in accordance with paragraph 1 of this article, the dossiers and other documentation relating to the cases referred to them.

Chapter III. Written proceedings

ARTICLE 7

1 Applications instituting proceedings shall be submitted to the Tribunal through the Executive Secretary in any one of the official languages of the United Nations. Such applications shall be divided into four sections, which shall be entitled respectively:

   I Information concerning the personal and official status of the applicant;

  II Pleas;

 III Explanatory statement;

 IV Annexes.

2 The information concerning the personal and official status of the applicant shall be presented in the form contained in annex I to these rules.

3 The pleas shall indicate all the measures and decisions which the applicant is requesting the Tribunal to order or take. They shall specify:

(a) Any preliminary or provisional measures, such as the production of additional documents or the hearing of witnesses, which the applicant is requesting the Tribunal to order before proceeding to consider the merits;

(b) The decisions which the applicant is contesting and whose rescission he is requesting under article 9, paragraph 1, of the Statute;

(c) The obligations which the applicant is invoking and whose specific performance he is requesting under article 9, paragraph 1, of the Statute;

(d) The amount of compensation claimed by the applicant in the event that the Secretary-General decides, in the interest of the United Nations, to pay compensation for the injury sustained in accordance with the option given to him under article 9, paragraph 1, of the Statute;

(e) And any other relief which the applicant may request in accordance with the Statute.

4 The explanatory statement shall set out the facts and the legal grounds

on which the pleas are based. It shall specify, *inter alia*, the provisions of the contract of employment or of the terms of appointment whose non-observance is alleged.

5 The annexes shall contain the texts of all documents referred to in the first three sections of the application. They shall be presented by the applicant in accordance with the following rules:

(a) Each document shall be annexed in the original or, failing that, in the form of a copy bearing the words "Certified true copy";

(b) Documents which are not in any of the official languages of the United Nations shall be accompanied by a translation into one of the working languages of the United Nations General Assembly;

(c) Each document, regardless of its nature, shall be annexed in its entirety, even if the application refers to only part of the document;

(d) Each document shall constitute a separate annex and shall be numbered with an Arabic numeral. The word "ANNEX", followed by the number of the document, shall appear at the top of the first page;

(e) The last annexed document shall be followed by a table of contents indicating the number, title, nature, date and, where appropriate, symbol of each annex;

(f) The words "see annex", followed by the appropriate number, shall appear in parentheses after each reference to an annexed document in the other sections of the application.

6 The applicant shall prepare seven copies of the application. Each copy shall contain a statement certifying that it is a true copy of the original application. It shall reproduce all sections of the original, including the annexes. However, the Executive Secretary may grant the applicant permission, at his request, to omit the text of an annex of unusual length from a specified number of copies of the application.

7 The applicant shall sign the last page of the original application and, in the annexes thereto, each certification made in accordance with paragraph 5 (a) above. He shall also sign, on each copy of the application, the statement referred to in paragraph 6 above. In the event of the applicant's incapacity, the required signatures shall be furnished by his legal representative. The applicant may also, by means of a letter transmitted for that purpose to the Executive Secretary, authorize his counsel or the staff member who is representing him to sign in his stead.

8 The applicant shall file the duly signed original and seven copies of the application with the Executive Secretary. Where the Secretary-General and the applicant have agreed to submit the application directly to the Tribunal in accordance with the option given to them under article 7, paragraph 1, of the Statute, the filing shall take place within ninety days of the date on which the Secretary-General notifies the applicant of his agreement to direct submission. In all other cases, the filing shall take place within the time limits prescribed by article 7, paragraph 4, of the Statute and by article 22 of these rules.

9 The time limits specified in the preceding paragraph shall be extended to one year in the case of an application filed by:

(a) Any person who has succeeded to the staff member's rights on his death; or

(b) The legal representative of a staff member who is not in a position to manage his own affairs.

10 If the formal requirements of this article are not fulfilled, the Executive Secretary may call upon the applicant to make the necessary corrections in the application and the copies thereof within a period which he shall prescribe. He shall return the necessary papers to the applicant for this purpose. He may also, with the approval of the President, make the necessary corrections himself when the defects in the application do not affect the substance.

11 After ascertaining that the requirements of this article are complied with, the Executive Secretary shall transmit a copy of the application to the respondent.

ARTICLE 8

1 The respondent's answer shall be submitted to the Tribunal through the Executive Secretary in any one of the working languages of the United Nations General Assembly. The answer shall include pleas, an explanatory statement and annexes. The annexes shall contain the complete texts of all documents referred to in the other sections of the answer. They shall be presented in accordance with the rules established for the application in article 7, paragraph 5. The number given to the first annex of the answer shall be the number following that given to the last annex of the application.

2 The respondent shall prepare seven copies of the answer. Each copy shall contain a statement certifying that it is a true copy of the original answer. It shall reproduce all sections of the original, including the annexes. However, the Executive Secretary may grant the respondent permission, at his request, to omit the text of an annex of unusual length from a specified number of copies of the answer.

3 The representative of the respondent shall sign the last page of the original answer and, in the annexes thereto, each certification made in accordance with article 7, paragraph 5 (a). He shall also sign, on each copy of the answer, the statement referred to in paragraph 2 above.

4 Within thirty days of the date on which the application is transmitted to him by the Executive Secretary, the respondent shall file the duly signed original and seven copies of the answer with the Executive Secretary.

5 After ascertaining that the requirements of this article are complied with, the Executive Secretary shall transmit a copy of the answer to the applicant.

ARTICLE 9

1 The applicant may, within thirty days of the date on which the answer is transmitted to him, file with the Executive Secretary written observations on the answer.

2 The complete text of any document referred to in the written observations shall be annexed thereto in accordance with the rules established for

the application in article 7, paragraph 5. The number given to the first annex of the written observations shall be the number following that given to the last annex of the answer.

3 The written observations shall be filed in an original and seven copies drawn up in accordance with the rules established for the application in article 7, paragraph 6. The original and the seven copies shall be signed in accordance with the rules established for the application in article 7, paragraph 7.

4 After ascertaining that the requirements of this article are complied with, the Executive Secretary shall transmit a copy of the written observations to the respondent.

ARTICLE 10

1 The President may, on his own initiative, or at the request of either party, call upon the parties to submit additional written statements or additional documents within a period which he shall fix. The additional documents shall be furnished in the original or in properly authenticated form. The written statements and additional documents shall be accompanied by seven properly authenticated copies. Any document not drawn up in any of the official languages of the United Nations shall be accompanied by a certified translation into one of the working languages of the General Assembly.

2 Each written statement and additional document shall be communicated by the Executive Secretary, on receipt, to the other parties, unless at the request of one of the parties and with the consent of the other parties, the Tribunal decides otherwise.

The personnel files communicated to the Tribunal shall be made available to the applicant by the Executive Secretary in accordance with instructions issued by the Tribunal.

3 In order to complete the documentation of the case prior to its being placed on the list, the President may obtain any necessary information from any party, witnesses or experts. The President may designate a member of the Tribunal or any other disinterested person to take oral statements. Any such statement shall be made under declaration as provided in article 16, paragraph 2.

4 The President may in particular cases delegate his functions under this article to one of the Vice-Presidents.

ARTICLE 11

1 When the President considers the documentation of a case to be sufficiently complete, he shall instruct the Executive Secretary to place the case on the list. The Executive Secretary shall inform the parties as soon as the inclusion of the case in the list is effected.

2 As soon as the date of opening of the session at which a case has been entered for hearing has been fixed, the Executive Secretary shall notify the date to the parties.

3 Any application for the adjournment of a case shall be decided by the President, or, when the Tribunal is in session, by the Tribunal.

ARTICLE 12

1 The Executive Secretary shall be responsible for transmitting all documents and making all notifications required in connection with proceedings before the Tribunal.

2 The Executive Secretary shall make for each case a dossier which shall record all actions taken in connexion with the preparation of the case for trial, the dates thereof, and the dates on which any document or notification forming part of the procedure is received in or despatched from his office.

ARTICLE 13

An applicant may present his case before the Tribunal in person, in either the written or oral proceedings. Subject to article 7 of these rules, he may designate a staff member of the United Nations or one of the specialized agencies so to represent him, or may be represented by counsel authorized to practice in any country a member of the organization concerned.

ARTICLE 14

The President may, when a party claims that he is unable to comply with the requirements of any rule in this chapter, waive such rule if the waiver does not affect the substance of the application.

Chapter IV. Oral proceedings

ARTICLE 15

1 Oral proceedings shall be held if the presiding member so decides or if either party so requests and the presiding member agrees. The oral proceedings may include the presentation and examination of witnesses or experts. Each party shall in addition have the right of oral argument and of comment on the evidence given.

2 In sufficient time before the opening of the oral proceedings, each party shall inform the Executive Secretary and, through him, the other parties, of the names and description of witnesses and experts whom he desires to be heard, indicating the points to which the evidence is to refer.

3 The Tribunal shall determine the sequence of oral proceedings. The parties shall, however, retain the right to comment briefly on any statement to which they have not replied.

ARTICLE 16

1 The Tribunal may examine the witnesses and experts. The parties, their representatives or counsel may, under the control of the presiding member, put questions to the witnesses and experts.

2 Each witness shall make the following declaration before giving his evidence:

"I solemnly declare upon my honour and conscience that I will speak the truth, the whole truth and nothing but the truth."

Each expert shall make the following declaration before making his statement:

"I solemnly declare upon my honour and conscience that my statement will be in accordance with my sincere belief."

3 The Tribunal may exclude evidence which it considers irrelevant, frivolous, or lacking in probative value. The Tribunal may also limit the oral testimony where it considers the written documentation adequate.

Chapter V. Additional documentation during the proceedings
ARTICLE 17

The Tribunal may at any stage of the proceedings call for the production of documents or of such other evidence as may be required. It may arrange for any measures of inquiry as may be necessary.

Chapter VI. Remand of a case under article 9, paragraph 2, of the Statute
ARTICLE 18

1 If, in the course of the deliberations, the Tribunal finds that the case be remanded in order that the required procedure may be instituted or corrected under article 9, paragraph 2, of the Statute, it shall notify the parties accordingly.

2 The Tribunal shall decide on the substance of the case if, on the expiry of the time limit of two days reckoned from the date of this notification, no request for a remand has been made by the Secretary-General.

Chapter VII. Intervention
ARTICLE 19

1 Any person to whom the Tribunal is open under article 2, paragraph 2, and article 14 of the Statute may apply to intervene in a case at any stage thereof on the ground that he has a right which may be affected by the judgement to be given by the Tribunal. He shall for that purpose draw up and file an application in form of annex II for intervention in accordance with the conditions laid down in this article.

2 The rules regarding the preparation and submission of applications specified in chapter III shall apply *mutatis mutandis* to the application for intervention.

3 After ascertaining that the requirements of the present article are complied with, the Executive Secretary shall transmit a copy of the application for intervention to the applicant and to the respondent. The President shall decide which documents, if any, relating to the proceedings are to be transmitted to the intervener by the Executive Secretary.

4 The Tribunal shall rule on the admissibility of every application for intervention submitted under this article.

ARTICLE 20

The Secretary-General of the United Nations, the chief administrative officer of a specialized agency to which the competence of the Tribunal has been extended in accordance with the Statute, or the Chairman of the

Joint Staff Pension Board, may, on giving previous notice to the President of the Tribunal, intervene at any stage, if they consider that their respective administrations may be affected by the judgement to be given by the Tribunal.

ARTICLE 21

When it appears that a person may have an interest to intervene in a case under articles 19 or 20, the President, or the Tribunal when in session, may instruct the Executive Secretary to transmit to such person a copy of the application submitted in the case.

Chapter VIII. Applications alleging non-observance of the Regulations of the United Nations Joint Staff Pension Fund

ARTICLE 22

Where an application is brought against a decision of the United Nations Joint Staff Pension Board or of the Staff Pension Committee of a member organization, the time limits prescribed in article 7 of the Statute are reckoned from the date of the communication of the contested decision to the party concerned.

Chapter IX. Miscellaneous provisions

ARTICLE 23

1 The Tribunal may grant a hearing, for purposes of information, to persons to whom the Tribunal is open under paragraph 2 of article 2 of the Statute even though they are not parties to the case, whenever such persons may be expected to furnish information pertinent to the case.

2 The Tribunal may, in its discretion, grant a hearing to duly authorized representatives of the staff association of the organization concerned.

ARTICLE 24

The Tribunal or, in the interval between its sessions, the President or the presiding member may shorten or extend any time limit fixed by these rules.

ARTICLE 25

The Executive Secretary shall send twice a year to all members of the Tribunal copies of all the decisions of the Tribunal during the preceding period.

ARTICLE 26

All matters which are not expressly provided for in the present rules shall be dealt with by decision of the Tribunal upon the particular case, by virtue of the powers conferred on it by article 6 of the Statute.

ANNEX I

Form of first section of application drawn up in accordance with article 7

INFORMATION CONCERNING THE PERSONAL AND OFFICIAL STATUS
OF THE APPLICANT

1 Designation of respondent.
2 Designation of applicant:
  (a) Name and first names;
  (b) Date and place of birth;
  (c) Marital status;
  (d) Nationality;
  (e) Address for purposes of the proceedings.
3 Designation, as appropriate, of counsel or staff member representing the applicant before the Tribunal.
4 Official status of applicant:
  (a) Organization of which the applicant was a staff member at the time of the decision contested;
  (b) Date of employment;
  (c) Title and grade at time of decision contested;
  (d) Type of applicant's contract.[a]
5 If the applicant was not a staff member at the time of the contested decision, state:
  (a) The name, first names, nationality and official status of the staff member whose rights are relied on;
  (b) The relation of the applicant to the said staff member which entitles the former to come before the Tribunal.
6 The date of the recommendation[a] of the joint appeals body relating to the dispute in question.
7 If the recommendation of the joint appeals body was favourable to the applicant, state either:
  (a) The date of the communication[a] in which the Secretary-General notified the applicant of his rejection of the recommendation; or
  (b) In case there has been no rejection, the date of the communication[a] in which the recommendation of the joint body was notified to the applicant.
8 If the recommendation of the joint body was unfavourable to the applicant, state:
  (a) The date of the communication[a] in which the recommendation was notified to the applicant;
  (b) The date of the communication[a] in which the Secretary-General's acceptance of the recommendation was notified to the applicant.
9 If the joint appeals body did not hear the dispute, state either:

---

[a] Indicate between brackets the number of the annex reproducing the relevant document in pursuance of paragraph 5 of article 7.

(a) The date of the decision[a] referred to in article 22 of the rules and the date of the communication[a] in which the decision was notified to the applicant; or

(b) The date of the communication[a] in which the applicant was notified of the Secretary-General's agreement to direct submission of the dispute to the Tribunal.

ANNEX II

Form of first section of application for intervention drawn up in accordance with article 19

INFORMATION CONCERNING THE PERSONAL AND OFFICIAL STATUS
OF THE INTERVENER

1 Case in which intervention is sought.
2 Designation of intervener:
   (a) Name and first names;
   (b) Date and place of birth;
   (c) Marital status;
   (d) Nationality;
   (e) Address for purposes of the proceedings.
3 Designation, as appropriate, of counsel or staff member representing the intervener before the Tribunal.
4 Official status of intervener:
   (a) Organization of which the intervener is a staff member;
   (b) Date of employment;
   (c) Title and grade;
   (d) Type of applicant's contract.[a]
5 In case of intervention under article 6, paragraph 2 (d) of the Statute, the intervener shall state:
   (a) The name, first names, nationality and official status of the staff member whose rights are relied on;
   (b) The title under which the intervener claims he is entitled to the rights of the said staff member.[a]

---

[a]Indicate between brackets the number of the annex reproducing the relevant document in pursuance of paragraph 5 of article 7.

NOTES

INTRODUCTION
1 Inis L. Claude, Jr., *Swords into Plowshare: The Problems and Progress of International Organization* (2nd ed.; New York: Random House, 1959), 193.
2 Suzanne Bastid, "Les Tribunaux Administratifs Internationaux et Leur Jurisprudence," *Recueil des cours*, XCII, Pt. 2 (1957), 347–517.
3 Suzanne Bastid, "Statut Juridique des Fonctionnaires des Nations Unies," in G. H. J. Van Der Molen, W. P. J. Pompe, and J. H. W. Verziji (eds.), *The United Nations: Ten Years' Legal Process* (Hague: Nederlandse Studentenvereniging voor Wereldrechtsorde, 1956), 145–65.
4 C. Wilfred Jenks, *The Proper Law of International Organisations* (London: Stevens & Sons Limited, 1962). The quoted passage is from the Preface, xv.
5 *Ibid.*, xxxiii–xxxiv.
6 Wolfgang Friedmann and Arghyrios A. Fatouros, "The United Nations Administrative Tribunal," *International Organization*, XI (1957), 13–29.
7 Philip C. Jessup, *Transnational Law* (New Haven: Yale University Press, 1956), 82–94.
8 Mohammed Bedjaoui, *Fonction Publique Internationale et Influences Nationales* (London: Stevens & Sons Ltd., 1958; Woonsang Choi, "The Legal Regulation of Employment Relations within International Organizations" (J. S. D. dissertation, Harvard University, 1960).
9 Herbert W. Briggs, "New Dimensions in International Law," *American Political Science Review*, XLVI (1952), 698. Briggs had borrowed the term "social fabric" from Hans J. Morgenthau, who, referring to the "peace, order, and prosperity of the Victorian age," said that: "It was because of the order existing in the *social fabric* that the orderly processes of the rule of law could give normative directions to social activities, not vice versa." (Italics mine.)
10 Inis Claude, Jr., "The United Nations and the Use of Force," *International Conciliation*, No. 532 (1951), 384.
11 In a lecture on American foreign policy, Cornell University, March, 1963.
12 United Nations, *Charter*, Art. 101, par. 3.

CHAPTER 1
1 United Nations, *Charter*, Art. 97, and Art. 101, par. 1.
2 United Nations, *Staff Regulations*, Scope and Purpose.

147

3 Sydney D. Bailey, *The Secretariat of the United Nations* (New York: Carnegie Endowment for International Peace, 1962), 74–75.
4 One of the seven main committees of the General Assembly. The others are: the First (Political and Security), Second (Economic and Financial), Third (Social, Humanitarian, and Cultural), Fourth (Trusteeship), Sixth (Legal), and Special Political Committees.
5 United Nations, *Charter*, Art. 101, par. 3.
6 United Nations, *Staff Regulations*, Regulation 4.3.
7 See Richard N. Swift, "Personnel Problems and the United Nations Secretariat," *International Organization*, XI (1957), 231.
8 Bailey, *Secretariat of the United Nations*, 91–93.
9 Peter Lengyel, "Some Trends in the International Civil Service," *International Organization*, XIII (1959), 522.
10 Bailey, *Secretariat of the United Nations*, 95–96.
11 Swift, "Personnel Problems," 229–30.
12 According to an experienced former international civil servant, these include: (1) understanding and consequential loyalty; (2) diplomatic capacity; (3) constructive imagination; (4) capacity for leadership; (5) *convivencia* (a Spanish word for which he says there is no English equivalent); (6) intellectual capacity; (7) administrative ability; (8) nervous energy; (9) determination; and (10) specialized knowledge. See A. Loveday, *Reflections on International Administration* (London: Oxford University Press, 1956), 32–38.
13 Swift, "Personnel Problems," 230.
14 *Ibid.*, 230–31.
15 Bailey, *Secretariat of the United Nations*, 103.
16 *Ibid.*, 103–104.
17 *Ibid.*, 105.
18 United Nations, *Staff Rules*, Rule 104.12.
19 *Ibid.*
20 *Ibid.*
21 *Ibid.*, Rule 104.13.
22 *Ibid.*
23 *Ibid.*, Rule 104.14.
24 United Nations, *Staff Regulations*, Salary Scales and Appendix B.
25 As of December 1962, there were 19 Under-Secretaries, 125 in the Principal Officer and Director Category, 1,831 in the Professional Category, and 2,303 in the General Service Category, The Secretariat thus had a total of 4,278 staff members on its payroll. See United Nations, General Assembly, *Budget Estimates for the Financial Year 1963: Report of the Fifth Committee* (A/5391, 19 December 1962), 28.
26 Dag Hammarskjöld, *The International Civil Servant in Law and in Fact* (London: Oxford University Press, 1961), 5.
27 United Nations, *Staff Regulations*, Regulation 1.2.
28 *Ibid.*, Regulation 1.3.
29 *Ibid.*, Regulation 1.4.
30 *Ibid.*
31 *Ibid.*, Regulation 1.5.
32 *Ibid.*, Regulation 1.6.
33 *Ibid.*, Regulation 1.7.
34 United Nations, *Staff Rules*, Rule 101.8.
35 Thus they do not enjoy diplomatic privileges and immunities in the international law sense, that is, in the sense that the privileges and immunities apply

both to official functions and to acts committed in a private capacity. Under Art. V, Section 18 of the General Convention on the Privileges and Immunities of the United Nations (1946), which, incidentally, has not been acceded to by the United States, officials of the United Nations shall:

(a) be immune from legal process in respect of words spoken or written and all acts performed by them in their official capacity;

(b) be exempt from taxation on the salaries and emoluments paid to them by the United Nations;

(c) be immune from national service obligations;

(d) be immune, together with their spouses and relatives dependent on them, from immigration restrictions and alien registration;

(e) be accorded the same privileges in respect of exchange facilities as are accorded to the officials of comparable ranks forming part of diplomatic missions to the government concerned;

(f) be given, together with their spouses and relatives dependent upon them, the same repatriation facilities in time of international crisis as diplomatic envoys;

(g) have the right to import free of duty their furniture and effects at the time of first taking up their post in the country in question.

See Herbert W. Briggs (ed.), *The Law of Nations: Cases, Documents, and Notes* (2nd. ed. (New York: Appleton-Century-Crofts, 1952), 796.

36 United Nations, *Staff Regulations*, Regulation 1.8.
37 For an excellent appraisal of the compensation practice in the United Nations, see A. Loveday, "Staff Salaries in the UN Family," *International Organization*, XI (1957), 635–48 and United Nations, General Assembly, *UN Salary, Allowances and Benefits Systems: Report of the Salary Review Committee* (A/3209, 18 October 1956).
38 Swift, "Personnel Problems," 237.
39 Gross salary less staff assessment.
40 United Nations, *Staff Regulations*, Salary Scales (as amended on 18 January 1962).
41 *Ibid.*, Regulation 8.1.
42 United Nations, *Staff Rules*, Rule 108.1.
43 United Nations, *Staff Regulations*, Regulation 8.2 and *Staff Rules*, Rule 108.2.
44 United Nations, *Staff Regulations*, Regulation 9.1(a).
45 United Nations, General Assembly, *Report of the Secretary-General on Personnel Policy* (A/2533, 2 November 1953), 15–16.
46 United Nations, General Assembly, *Personnel Policy: Reports of the Secretary-General and of the Advisory Committee on Administrative and Budgetary Questions* (Report of the Fifth Committee) (A/2615, 7 December 1953), 10–11.
47 United Nations, *Staff Regulations*, Regulation 9.1(b) and (c).
48 *Ibid.*, Regulations 9.3 and 9.4.
49 *Ibid.*, Regulation 10.2.
50 United Nations, *Staff Rules*, Rule 110.1, 2, and 3.
51 *Ibid.*, Rule 111.1.
52 *Ibid.*, Rule 111.2.
53 *Ibid.*, Rule 111.3(a).
54 *Ibid.*, Rule 111.3(b), (c), and (d).
55 *Ibid.*, Rule 111.3(e) and (1).
56 See Hans Gerth and C. Wright Mills (trans. & eds.), *From Max Weber: Essays in Sociology* (New York: Oxford University Press, 1946), pp. 202–203 and Max Weber, *The Theory of Social and Economic Organization,*

trans. A. M. Henderson and Talcott Parsons (New York: Oxford University Press, 1947), 333–34.

57 Gerth and Mills (tr. and eds.), *From Max Weber*, 202.

58 Frederick Herzberg et al, *Job Attitudes: Review of Research and Opinion* (Pittsburgh: Psychological Service of Pittsburgh, 1957), 41.

59 Morris S. Viteles, *Motivation and Morale in Industry* (New York: W. W. Norton & Co., 1953), 302–18. The quote is from pages 310–11.

60 *Ibid.*, 43–77. The quote is from page 76.

61 Frederick Herzberg, Bernard Mausner, and Barbara Block Snyderman, *The Motivation to Work* (2nd. ed.; New York: John Wiley and Sons, Inc., 1959), 50.

62 Nigel Walker, *Morale in the Civil Service: A Study of the Desk Worker* (Edinburgh: Edinburgh University Press, 1961), 34–56.

63 *Ibid.*, 34.

64 *Ibid.*, 34–35.

65 Dwaine Marvick, *Career Perspectives in a Bureaucratic Setting* (Ann Arbor: University of Michigan Press, 1954), 17–19.

66 Peter M. Blau, *The Dynamics of Bureaucracy: A Study of Interpersonal Relations in Two Governmental Agencies* (Chicago: University of Chicago Press, 1953), 207–208.

67 See Brian Chapman, *The Profession of Government* (London: George Allen & Unwin Ltd., 1959), 229; P. Chatenet, "The Civil Service in France," in William A. Robson (ed.), *The Civil Service in Britain and France* (London: The Hogart Press, 1956), 164–88; Alfred Diamant, "The French Administrative System: The Republic Passes but the Administration Remains," in William J. Siffin (ed.) *Toward the Comparative Study of Public Administration* (Bloomington: Department of Government, Indiana University, 1957), 202; Herman Finer, *Theory and Practice of Modern Government* (Rev. ed.; New York: Henry Holt & Co., 1950), 915 and *Governments of Greater European Powers* (New York: Henry Holt & Co., 1956), 312.

68 See G. A. Campbell, *The Civil Service in Britain* (Harmondsworth, Middlesex: Penguin Books Ltd., 1955), 283; E. N. Gladden, *Civil Service or Bureaucracy* (London: Staples Press Ltd., 1956), 48, 120; Walker, *Morale in Civil Service*, 34–56; and Harold Zink, *Modern Governments* (Princeton: D. Van Nostrand Co., Inc., 1958), 151.

69 See H. Eliot Kaplan, *The Law of Civil Service* (New York: Mathew Bender & Co., 1958), 225; O. Glenn Stahl, *Public Personnel Administration* (4th. ed.; New York: Harper, 1956), 464–72; U. S. Civil Service Commission, *Civil Service News* (news release), March 28, 1962 (Washington, 1962); and Paul P. Van Riper, *History of the United States Civil Service* (Evanston: Row, Peterson & Co., 1958), 99–102.

CHAPTER 2

1 Friedmann and Fatouros, "The United Nations Administrative Tribunal," 13.

2 Bastid, "Les Tribunaux Administratifs Internationaux," 348.

3 *Ibid.*, 349.

4 The term "international community" is used in a somewhat loose sense, for it is a matter of some debate whether the existing conglomeration of "sovereign" states can justifiably be called a "community" in its full sociological and anthropological senses. For the argument that ours is a grossly imperfect society, see Percy E. Corbett, *Law and Society in the Relations of States* (New York: Harcourt, Brace & Co., 1951) and Quincy Wright, *Contemporary In-*

ternational Law: A Balance Sheet (Rev. ed.; New York: Random House, 1961).

5 *Statute of the International Court of Justice*, Art. 65, par. 1 and Art. 34, par. 1.
6 Bastid, "Les Tribunaux Administratifs Internationaux," 347.
7 Manley O. Hudson, *International Tribunals: Past and Future* (New York: Carnegie Endowment for International Peace, 1944), 220.
8 Bastid, "Les Tribunaux Administratifs Internationaux," 364.
9 *Ibid.*, 369.
10 Bedjaoui, *Fonction Publique Internationale*, 425–26.
11 They were Messieurs Adlercreutz (Sweden), van Slooten (Netherlands), and Barone (Italy). Bastid, "Les Tribunaux Administratifs Internationaux," 370.
12 *Ibid.*
13 Bedjaoui, *Fonction Publique Internationale*, 426.
14 Tien-Chen Young, *International Civil Service: Principles and Problems* (Brussels: International Institute of Administrative Sciences, 1958), 190.
15 Bedjaoui, *Fonction Publique Internationale*, 427.
16 Bastid, "Les Tribunaux Administratifs Internationaux," 371 and Hudson, *International Tribunals*, 221.
17 Bastid, "Les Tribunaux Administratifs Internationaux," 372.
18 *Ibid.*, 373.
19 *Ibid.*, 373–374.
20 *Ibid.*, 375.
21 *Ibid.*
22 *Ibid.*, 376.
23 *Ibid.*
24 Hudson, *International Tribunals*, 221.
25 *Ibid.*, 221–22.
26 Bastid, "Les Tribunaux Administratifs Internationaux," 387–88.
27 Young, *International Civil Service*, 193.
28 *Ibid.*, 194.
29 Conference of the FAO, *Administrative Tribunal and Appeals Procedure: Extract from Report of Council of FAO: Seventh Session, 14–17 November 1949* (FAO C49/III/3, 21 November 1949), Appendix B, 9.
30 Woonsang Choi, "The Legal Regulation of Employment Relations within International Organizations," 12.
31 Young, *International Civil Service*, 193.
32 Bastid, "Les Tribunaux Administratifs Internationaux," 401.
33 *Ibid.*, 401–402.
34 Choi, "Legal Regulation of Employment Relations," 13.
35 Bastid, "Les Tribunaux Administratifs Internationaux," 402–403.
36 *Ibid.*, 403.
37 United Nations, Preparatory Commission, *Report of the Executive Committee* (PC/EX/113/Rev. 1, 12 November 1945), 83, 108.
38 United Nations, Preparatory Commission, *Administrative Tribunal: Report of Committee 6* (PC/AB/45, 15 December 1945), 1.
39 United Nations, Preparatory Commission, *Report of Committee 6* (PC/AB/56/Rev. 2, 22 December 1945), 6 and *passim.*
40 United Nations, General Assembly, *Administrative Tribunal: Report of the Secretary-General* (A/91, 16 October 1946), 1–2.
41 *Ibid.*, 2. All titles, unless otherwise indicated, refer to those held by the individuals as of October 16, 1946.

42 *Ibid.*, 3.
43 *Ibid.*
44 *Ibid.*, 9, 4.
45 *Ibid.*, 4.
46 *Ibid.*, 4–5.
47 *Ibid.*
48 *Ibid.*, 11.
49 *Ibid.*, 6, 11.
50 *Ibid.*, 12 (Art. 10).
51 *Ibid.*
52 *Ibid.*, 8.
53 United Nations, General Assembly, *Organization and Administration of the Secretariat: Report of the Fifth Committee* (A/273, 13 December 1946), 2.
54 United Nations, General Assembly, *Establishment of an Administrative Tribunal: Report of the Secretary-General* (A/986, 21 September 1949), 1.
55 *Ibid.*, 1–2.
56 *Ibid.*, 2.
57 *Ibid.*, 3.
58 Annex 4 (Memorandum From the Staff Committee with Respect to the Proposal for an Administrative Tribunal), *ibid.*, 22.
59 *Ibid.*, 23.
60 *Ibid.*, 26.
61 *Ibid.*
62 *Ibid.*, 27.
63 United Nations, General Assembly, *Establishment of an Administrative Tribunal: Fifth report of 1949 of the Advisory Committee on Administrative and Budgetary Questions* (A/1003, 28 September 1949), 1–2.
64 *Ibid.*, 2–3. Italics mine.
65 *Ibid.*, 3.
66 United Nations, General Assembly, *Establishment of Administrative Tribunal: Note by Secretary-General* (A/C.5/304, 29 September 1949), 1–3. The quotation is from page 3.
67 United Nations, General Assembly, *Establishment of an Administrative Tribunal: Note Submitted by the WHO* (A/C.5/L.21, 2 November 1949), 1–2.
68 United Nations, General Assembly, *Establishment of an Administrative Tribunal: Draft Report of the Fifth Committee* (A/C.5/L.41, 21 November 1949), 1.
69 United Nations, General Assembly, *Establishment of an Administrative Tribunal: Report of the Fifth Committee* (A/1127, 22 November 1949), 2.
70 *Ibid.*, 2–3.
71 *Ibid.*, 3–4.
72 United Nations, General Assembly, Fifth Committee, *Provisional Summary Record* (A/C.5/SR 187, 188, 189, 190, 214, 215, 216, and 221; 29 September to 8 November 1949), *passim.* The summary of the various positions taken by these delegations which follows is also based on the same sources.
73 United Nations, General Assembly, *Establishment of an Administrative Tribunal: Belgium, Egypt, France, Netherlands, Venezuela: Amendments to the draft statute of the Administrative Tribunal proposed by the Fifth Committee* (A/1127) (A/1132, 23 November 1949), 1.
74 United Nations, General Assembly, *Verbatim Record of the 255th Plenary Meeting, Fourth Session* (A/PV 255, 24 November 1949), 20–21.
75 United Nations, General Assembly, *Establishment of a United Nations Administrative Tribunal: Resolution adopted by the General Assembly at its 255th plenary meeting on November 24, 1949* (A/1142, 25 November 1949), 1–2.

76 United Nations, General Assembly, *Verbatim Record of the 274th Plenary Meeting, Fourth Session,* (A/PV 274, 9 December 1949), 6–10. For biographical data, see United Nations, General Assembly, *Establishment of an Administrative Tribunal: Appointment of Members* (A/C.5/L.45, 5 December 1949), 1–3.

77 United Nations, General Assembly, *Official Records: Sixth Session,* Supplement No. 1 (Annual Report of the Secretary-General on the Work of the Organization, 1 July 1949–30 June 1950) (A/1287, 1950), 140.

CHAPTER 3

1 "Judgments of the Administrative Tribunal of the I.L.O. upon complaints made against the UNESCO, Advisory Opinion of October 23rd, 1956," *I.C.J. Reports 1956,* 97. Also quoted in French in Bastid, "Les Tribunaux Administratifs Internationaux," 405.

2 Mme. Bastid thus uses the term "des jurisdictions internationales," which she defines as "des jurisdictions qui règlent des litiges qui dépassent le cadre de l'Etat." Bastid, "Les Tribunaux Administratifs Internationaux," 405.

3 "Effect of awards of compensation made by the U.N. Administrative Tribunal, Advisory Opinion of July 13th, 1954," *I.C.J. Reports 1954,* 58. The events which led to the request of the advisory opinion, together with its contents and significance, are discussed in Chapter V.

4 Bastid, "Les Tribunaux Administratifs Internationaux," 408.

5 *Ibid.*

6 *I.C.J. Reports 1954,* 51–53.

7 *Ibid.,* 51.

8 *Ibid.,* 52.

9 *Ibid.,* 52–53.

10 *Ibid.,* 53. The World Court's opinion regarding the legal status of the Tribunal receives further attention later in the study in connection with the discussion of the so-called "political" cases. See Chapter VI, *infra.*

11 United Nations, *Statute of the Administrative Tribunal,* Art. 3, pars. 1 and 2.

12 United Nations, General Assembly, *Adoption of the Agenda of the Seventeenth Regular Session, Allocation of Items, and Organization of the Session: First report of the General Committee* (A/5230, 21 September 1962), 8, 20.

13 United Nations, General Assembly, *Appointments to Fill Vacancies in the Membership of Subsidiary Bodies of the General Assembly: United Nations Administrative Tribunal* (Report of the Fifth Committee) (A/5295, 29 November 1962), 1.

14 United Nations, General Assembly, *Appointments to Fill Vacancies in the Membership of Subsidiary Bodies of the General Assembly: Administrative Tribunal* (Note by the Secretariat) (A/C.5/L.752 and 753, 21 November 1962).

15 A/5295, p. 3.

16 The summary fashion in which the General Assembly adopts such resolutions is suggested by the following excerpts from verbatim records:

The PRESIDENT: With Regard to the membership of the United Nations Administrative Tribunal, the Fifth Committee has made its recommendations in document A/5295. If there is no objection, I shall take it that the draft resolution is adopted.

[There being no objections] *The draft resolution contained in document A/5295 was adopted.*

See United Nations, General Assembly, *Provisional Verbatim Records of the Eleven Hundred and Ninety-First Plenary Meeting, Seventeenth Session* (A/PV.1191, 11 December 1962), 12.

17 United Nations, General Assembly, *Budget Estimates for the Financial Year 1961: Payment of honorarium to members of the Administrative Tribunal* (Report of the Secretary-General) (A/C.5/814, 4 May 1960), 1.

18 *Ibid.*, 1–2.

19 *Ibid.*, 2–3.

20 *Ibid.*, annex 1, p. 1.

21 United Nations, General Assembly, *Official Records: Fifteenth Session,* Supplement No. 7 (Advisory Committee on Administrative and Budgetary Questions, First Report to the General Assembly at Its Fifteenth Session) (A/4408, 1960), 41–42.

22 United Nations, General Assembly, *Budget Estimates for the Financial Year 1961: Payment of honoraria to the members of the Administrative Tribunal* (Report of the Fifth Committee) (A/4609, 2 December 1960), 1–2.

23 *Ibid.*, 3–4.

24 "Reparation for injuries suffered in the service of the United Nations, Advisory Opinion," *I.C.J. Reports 1949*, 177.

25 Bastid, "Les Tribunaux Administratifs Internationaux," 411. Article VI of the Convention provides in part that experts performing missions for the United Nations shall be accorded "such privileges and immunities as are necessary for the independent exercise of their functions during the period of their missions, including the time spent on journeys in connection with their missions." See Briggs (ed.), *The Law of Nations* 796–97.

26 United Nations, *Statute of the Administrative Tribunal,* Art. 3, par. 5.

27 United Nations, General Assembly, *Report of the Committee on Special Administrative Questions: Report of the Fifth Committee* (A/2539, 2 November 1953), 2.

28 Bastid, "Les Tribunaux Administratifs Internationaux," 410.

29 United Nations, *Statute of the Administrative Tribunal,* Art. 3, par. 1.

30 Bastid, "Les Tribunaux Administratifs Internationaux," 411.

31 This, I hasten to add, is not to imply that members of the Tribunal are representatives of their states. Far from it. The members serve in their individual capacities and as impartial and independent judges.

32 United Nations, *Rules of the Administrative Tribunal,* Art. 2.

33 *Ibid.*, Art. 3.

34 United Nations, *Statute of the Administrative Tribunal,* Art. 3, par. 4.

35 *Ibid.*, Art. 5, par. 1.

36 Not capitalized so that it may be distinguished from the Secretariat of the United Nations.

37 Interviews with the Executive Secretary of the United Nations Administrative Tribunal, December, 1962, and April, 1963.

38 *Ibid.*

39 United Nations, *Statute of the Administrative Tribunal,* Art. 5, par. 2.

CHAPTER 4

1 Shabtai Rosenne, *The International Court of Justice: An Essay in Political and Legal Theory* (Leyden, the Netherlands: A. W. Sijthoff's Uitgeversmaatschappij N.V., 1957), 253.

2 See, for example, Art. 2, pars. 1, 3, and 4 and Art. 14. The word "jurisdiction" appears only twice, both in Art. 11, par. 1.

3 See Art. 36.

4 Rosenne, *The International Court of Justice,* 252–53.

5 *I.C.J. Reports 1954*, 57–58.

6 *Ibid.*, 56. For a further exposition of the legal meaning of jurisdiction, with

particular, but by no means exclusive, reference to the International Court of Justice, see Rosenne, *International Court of Justice,* 253–77.

7 Hudson, *International Tribunals,* 67.

8 Hudson chose "to deal with problems of the first category as including the general subject of access to tribunals, and with those of the second category as relating to jurisdiction in a narrower sense of the term." *Ibid.*

9 United Nations, *Statute of the Administrative Tribunal,* Art. 2, par. 2.

10 Bastid, "Les Tribunaux Administratifs Internationaux," 446–47.

11 Chap. XV, The Secretariat.

12 *I.C.J. Reports 1949,* 184–85. The Court said in part that "fifty States, representing the vast majority of the members of the international community, had the power, in conformity with international law, to bring into being an entity possessing objective international personality and not merely personality recognized by them alone, together with capacity to bring international claims." *Ibid.,* 185. See also *I.C.J. Reports 1954,* 53.

13 An exceptional case where a former Secretary-General of the League brought a suit before the I.L.O. Tribunal, however, is reported by Mme. Bastid. In that case, Joseph Avenol, former Secretary-General of the League, had alleged a violation of his pension rights. Bastid, "Les Tribunaux Administratifs Internationaux," 446.

14 *Ibid.*

15 *Ibid.,* 447–48.

16 United Nations, *Statute of the Administrative Tribunal,* Art. 2, par. 2(a).

17 Bastid, "Les Tribunaux Administratifs Internationaux," 451.

18 United Nations, General Assembly, *Acceptance by the Specialized Agencies of the Jurisdiction of the United Nations Administrative Tribunal in Matters Involving Applications Alleging Non–observance of the Regulations of the United Nations Joint Staff Pension Fund: Report of Secretary–General* (A/2970, 19 September 1955), Annex page 2.

19 *Ibid.*

20 *Hilpern* v. *United Nations Relief and Works Agency for Palestine Refugees in the Near East,* 57 JUNAT 304 (1955). JUNAT refers to *Judgments of the United Nations Administrative Tribunal,* Numbers 1 to 70, 1950–1957 (AT/DEC/1 to 70, 1958). The Judgment number precedes the abbreviated title, and page number and date follow. Except where otherwise indicated, the respondent is the Secretary–General of the United Nations. The applicant's name appears in the beginning.

21 *Hilpern,* 57 JUNAT 296 (1955); *Hilpern,* 63 JUNAT 350 (1956); *Radico-poulos* v. *United Nations Relief and Works Agency for Palestine Refugees in the Near East,* 70 JUNAT 419 (1957); and *Puvrez* v. *The Secretary–General of the International Civil Aviation Organization* (AT/DEC/82, 4 December 1961). A different method of citation is used for Judgments Nos. 71 to 90, because they have not yet been compiled in a single volume.

22 United Nations, *Statute of the Administrative Tribunal,* Art. 2, par. 1.

23 *Ibid.,* Art. 2, par. 4.

24 As Manley O. Hudson wrote, "It would serve little purpose to permit a challenge of jurisdiction to be made before a tribunal unless the tribunal had the power to construe the attributions of its competence, and to give decisions with reference to them which would be binding on the parties." Hudson, *International Tribunals,* 72. See also *Statute of the International Court of Justice,* Art. 36, par. 6.

25 United Nations, *Statute of the Administrative Tribunal,* Art. 2, par. 3.

26 *Wallach,* 28 JUNAT 117–119 (1953).

27 *Hilpern* v. *United Nations Relief and Works Agency for Palestine Refugees in the Near East,* 57 JUNAT 302–306 (1955).

28 *Radicopoulos* v. *United Nations Relief and Works Agency for Palestine Refugees in the Near East,* 70 JUNAT 428 (1957).

29 United Nations, Administrative Tribunal, *Competence of the Tribunal to Award Costs: Memorandum submitted by the Legal Department* (A/CN.5/5, 13 December 1950), 2.

30 *Glassman,* 33 JUNAT 159 (1953).

31 *Crawford et al.,* 61 JUNAT 335 (1955).

32 *Ibid.,* 336.

33 "Procedure in international tribunals," wrote Hudson, "is characterized predominantly by its flexibility, even by its informality." He continued: "Unlike the procedure in some national courts, it has not been congealed within the confines of strict and rigid rules. There are no traps into which an unwary litigant may innocently fall, mistakes are readily condoned, and penalties are seldom imposed." Hudson, *International Tribunals,* 84.

34 Art. 7, par. 1.

35 United Nations, *Statute of the Administrative Tribunal,* Art. 7, par. 2.

36 *Ibid.,* Art. 7, par. 3.

37 *Ibid.,* Art. 7, par. 4.

38 *Ibid.,* Art. 7, pars. 4, 5, and 6.

39 United Nations, *Rules of the Administrative Tribunal,* Art. 7, pars. 1 and 2.

40 *Ibid.,* Art. 7, par. 3.

41 *Ibid.,* Art. 7, pars. 4 and 5.

42 *Ibid.,* Art. 7, pars. 6, 7, and 8.

43 *Ibid.,* Art. 7, pars. 9 and 10.

44 United Nations, *Statute of the Administrative Tribunal,* Art. 7, par. 6.

45 See *Vanhove,* 13 JUNAT 36 (1952) and *Mauch,* 54 JUNAT 271–272 (1954).

46 *Ibid.,* Art. 8.

47 *Ibid.,* Art. 9.

48 *Ibid.,* Art. 10.

49 *Ibid.,* Art. 11, par. 1.

50 According to Rosenne, seisin refers to "the validity of the formal step by which the proceedings were instituted." Rosenne, *International Court of Justice,* 257–59.

51 United Nations, *Rules of the Administrative Tribunal,* Art. 11, par. 2.

52 *Ibid.,* Art. 12.

53 *Ibid.,* Art. 13.

54 United Nations, Secretariat, *Representation by Counsel in Disciplinary and Appeals Cases: An Administrative Instruction issued by the Secretary-General to members of the Staff* (ST/AI/153, 7 March 1963), 1–2.

55 *Ibid.,* 2–3.

56 United Nations, Secretariat, *Membership of the Panel of Counsel in Disciplinary and Appeal Cases: An Information Circular issued by the Director of Personnel to members of the staff* (ST/ADM/SER.A/833, 7 March 1963).

57 United Nations, *Rules of the Administrative Tribunal,* Art. 14.

58 United Nations, General Assembly, *Note by the Secretary-General* (A/INF/52, 30 December 1952), 3.

59 They had been revised once—in 1951. In other words, there have been five revisions to the Rules since the inception of the Tribunal.

60 United Nations, *Rules of the Administrative Tribunal,* Art. 15, par. 1.

61 The declaration to be made by each witness reads: "I solemnly declare upon my honour and conscience that I will speak the truth, the whole truth and

nothing but the truth." Each expert must declare: "I solemnly declare upon my honour and conscience that my statement will be in accordance with my sincere belief." *Ibid.*, Art. 16, par. 2.

62 *Ibid.*, Art. 15, par. 3 and Art. 16, par. 3; and United Nations, *Statute of the Administrative Tribunal*, Art. 8.

63 During the consideration of the so-called "political cases"—the cases involving the loyalty investigations of staff-members of U.S. nationality—, however, the system of consecutive, rather than simultaneous, translation was used. Interview with the Executive Secretary of the United Nations Administrative Tribunal, April, 1963.

64 United Nations, Administrative Tribunal, *Verbatim Records* (Restricted; A/CN.5/PV.1–4 and AT/PV/5–86, 1950–1962), *passim.* The suggestion that counsel be addressed as "my friend opposite" was first made by a President of the Tribunal in 1950. The President, His Highness Maharaja Jam Saheb of Nawanagar (India), said: ". . . I sincerely hope we will not hear the words "my opponent" or "adversary" and in future it will be "my friend opposite," or what lawyers have a very curious habit of calling "my honourable friend opposite." But still I think I want to introduce the atmosphere where we do not want opponents; we all belong to the same show." *Idem, Verbatim Records* (A/CN.5/PV.4, 30 June 1950), 69.

65 United Nations, *Rules of the Administrative Tribunal*, Art. 17.

66 *Miss X* (AT/DEC/81, 10 November 1960), 10.

67 United Nations, *Statute of the Administrative Tribunal*, Art. 9, par. 2 and *Rules of the Administrative Tribunal*, Art. 18.

68 *Wallach*, 28 JUNAT 119 (1953).

69 *Bertrand*, 59 JUNAT 320–321 (1955).

70 *Miss Y*, (AT/DEC/83, 8 December 1961), 10–11.

71 United Nations, *Rules of the Administrative Tribunal*, Art. 19.

72 *Ibid.*, Arts. 20 and 21.

73 *Aubert et al.*, 1 JUNAT 2 (1950).

74 *Aubert et al.*, 1 Addendum JUNAT 3 (1950).

75 United Nations, *Rules of the Administrative Tribunal*, Art. 23.

76 *Ibid.*, Arts. 25 and 26.

77 *Ibid.*, Art. 5, par. 1.

78 *Ibid.*, Art. 5, pars. 2, 3, and 4.

79 *Ibid.*, Art. 6, pars. 1 and 2 and Art. 3, par. 3.

80 *Ibid.*, Art. 6, pars. 3, 4, and 5.

81 Exactly how each decision of the Tribunal is arrived at could not be determined. The Executive Secretary classified such information as confidential.

82 United Nations, *Statute of the Administrative Tribunal*, Art. 10.

83 Hudson, *International Tribunals*, 113–14.

84 A standard format has been in use since 1953 (Judgment No. 18).

85 In Judgment No. 81, the Tribunal introduced the unusual practice of omitting the applicant's name from the published versions of the judgment "in view of the circumstances of the case." This practice was repeated in Judgment No. 83. In these cases, the applicants were designated as Misses X and Y, respectively. See AT/DEC/81, page 15 and AT/DEC/83, page 12.

86 Dissenting opinion on the Secretary-General's power to terminate temporary–indefinite contracts was appended by Rowland Egger in Judgment No. 4. Jacob M. Lashly wrote a separate opinion on termination of temporary–indefinite contracts in Judgment No. 60. Both members of the Tribunal are U. S. nationals.

87 Choi, "Legal Regulation of Employment Relations," 401.

88 Bastid, "Statut Juridique de Fonctionnaires des Nations Unies," in Van Der Molen, *et al.*, (eds.), *The United Nations Ten Years' Legal Progress*, 152.

89 Administrative law, as understood in American jurisprudence, is described by Hart as "the law that is *made by* as well as the law that *controls*, the administrative authorities of a government." James Hart, *An Introduction to Administrative Law: With Selected Cases* (New York: F. S. Crofts & Co., 1940), 3. Independent regulatory commissions, together with federal courts, play the key role in the making of such law. See, for example, Walter Gellhorn and Clark Byse, *Administrative Law: Cases and Comments* (Brooklyn: The Foundation Press, Inc., 1960). On the other hand, *droit administratif*, as developed in France, refers to the body of law applied by administrative tribunals in regulating practically all phases of the administrative process. See, for example, C. J. Hamson, *Executive Discretion and Judicial Control* (London: Stevens & Sons Ltd., and Benoit Jeanneau, *Les Principes Generaux du Droit dans la Jurisprudence Administrative* (Paris, 1954).

90 Hudson, *International Tribunals*, 99.

91 *Statute of the International Court of Justice*, Art. 38.

92 United Nations, *Statute of the Administrative Tribunal*, Art. 2, par. 1.

93 "The law governing the relations of international organisations with their officials, employees and agents," writes C. Wilfred Jenks, "consists primarily of the constitutional and administrative provisions of the organisations concerned and the contractual undertakings entered into between them and their servants and agents, as interpreted by the decisions of international administrative tribunals." He adds that municipal court decisions have made little contribution to its development. See Jenks, *The Proper Law of International Organisations*, 27.

94 United Nations, *Repertory of Practice of United Nations Organs*, vol. V (New York, 1955), 237–38.

95 United Nations, *Staff Regulations*, Annex II.

96 Bastid, "Statut Juridique de Fonctionnaires des Nations Unies," in Van Der Molen, et al., (eds.), *The United Nations Ten Years' Legal Progress*, 147–48. For a further exposition of the nature of contract, see Chapter VI, *infra*.

97 United Nations, *Staff Rules and Regulations*, table of contents.

98 For specific texts of the Staff Regulations and Rules mentioned in the Tribunal's judgments, see JUNAT, appendix, 437–45.

99 The Manual consists of four loose-leaf volumes—I. Organization, II. Personnel, III. Finance, and IV. Office Practice and Service—and is intended as "the official medium for the issuance of administrative policies, instructions and procedures designed to implement the Staff Rules, the Financial Rules and certain delegations of authority and responsibility which are, and will continue to be, issued in the Secretary-General's Bulletins." Its use, however, has been discontinued since 1957. See United Nations, Secretariat, *Administrative Manual* (UNST) (02) A2, n.d.).

100 See, for example, *Robinson*, 15 JUNAT 45 (1952); *Morrow*, 16 JUNAT 56 (1952); *Aglion*, 56 JUNAT 289 (1954); and *Russell-Cobb*, 55 JUNAT 278 (1954).

101 *Robinson*, 15 JUNAT 45–46 (1952).

102 *Russell-Cobb*, 55 JUNAT 278 (1954).

103 *Harris et al.*, 67 JUNAT 394–397 (1956).

104 The Executive Secretary of the Tribunal has referred to them as "our Bible." Informal conversations, April, 1963.

105 Bastid, "Les Tribunaux Administratifs Internationaux," 476. For evidence that the Statute and Rules are the frequent object of interpretation by the Tribunal, see JUNAT, index, 451.

106 While municipal courts, as a rule, refrain themselves from dealing with matters concerning the legal relations of international organizations with their employees, there have nevertheless been interesting cases in which, in the course of upholding immunity or declining jurisdiction, they have had occasion to comment on the nature of such legal relations and of the law governing them. See Jenks, *Proper Law of International Organisations*, 34–35.
107 *Hilpern* v. *United Nations Relief and Works Agency for Palestine Refugees in the Near East*, 63 JUNAT 363 (1956).
108 *Hilpern* v. *United Nations Relief and Works Agency for Palestine Refugees in the Near East*, 65 JUNAT 374 (1956).
109 *Khavkine,* 66 JUNAT 383 (1956).
110 *Stepczynski,* 64 JUNAT 372 (1956). That the Tribunal does not hesitate to rely on works of eminent scholars is also indicated in Judgments Nos. 11 and 12, where it cited McCormick's *Handbook on the Law of Damages.* See *Howrani,* 11 JUNAT 31 (1951) and *Keeney,* 12 JUNAT 34 (1951).
111 See JUNAT, index, 475.
112 *Robinson,* 15 JUNAT 47 (1952) and *Khavkine,* 66 JUNAT 379 (1956).
113 *Khavkine,* 66 JUNAT 388 (1956).
114 For specific examples of such principles, see Jenks, *Proper Law of International Organisations*, 51–62.
115 See Art. 38 of both *Statutes.*
116 Bastid, "Les Tribunaux Administratifs Internationaux," 479.
117 *Howrani et al.,* 4 JUNAT 17 (1951).
118 *Crawford et al.,* 61 JUNAT 336 (1955).
119 *Davidson* (AT/DEC/88, 3 October 1963), 10.
120 *Crawford,* 18 JUNAT 70 (1953). Repeated in later judgments.
121 *Howrani et al.,* 4 JUNAT 13–14, 17 (1951) and *Crawford et al.,* 61 JUNAT 336 (1955).
122 Bastid, "Les Tribunaux Administratifs Internationaux," 480.
123 *Aubert et al.,* 2 JUNAT 6 (1950).
124 *Keeney,* 12 JUNAT 35 (1951).
125 *Harris et al.,* 67 JUNAT 397 (1956).
126 *Bulsara* (AT/DEC/74, 5 December 1958), 13.
127 Bastid, "Les Tribunaux Administratifs Internationaux," 487.
128 See Jenks, *Proper Law of International Organisations,* 102–13.
129 *Howrani et al.,* 4 JUNAT 10 (1951).
130 See, for example, *Gordon,* 29 JUNAT 125 (1953); *Aglion,* 56 JUNAT 294 (1954); and *Stepczynski,* 64 JUNAT 367–370 (1956).
131 Quoted in *Howrani et al.,* 4 JUNAT 13–14 (1951).
132 United Nations, *Statute of the Administrative Tribunal,* Art. 9, par. 1.
133 *Ibid.*
134 *Eldridge,* 39 JUNAT 201 (1953). See also *Crawford,* 42 JUNAT 209 (1953).
135 *Howrani,* 11 JUNAT 31 (1951).
136 *Supra,* Ch. III.
137 United Nations, General Assembly, *Report of the Secretary-General on Personnel Policy* (A/2533, 2 November 1953), 27–28. Italics mine.
138 *Ibid.,* 28–29. It may be added parenthetically that the above amendment was a part of a package proposal in which the Secretary-General wanted also to liberalize the grounds for dismissal, adding such criteria as "integrity" and "the interest of the good administration of the Organization." This proposal was made against the backdrop of the celebrated "political" cases in which several Americans in the Secretariat who had been dismissed by the Secretary-General were ordered to be reinstated by the Tribunal. The Secretary-

General, however, chose to pay them compensation in lieu of reinstatement. For more details, see Chapter V, *infra.*

139 United Nations, General Assembly, *Personnel Policy of the United Nations: Note by the Secretary-General* (A/C.5/561, 16 November 1953), 11.

140 United Nations, General Assembly, *Personnel Policy: Reports of the Secretary-General and the Advisory Committee on Administrative and Budgetary Questions* (Report of the Fifth Committee) (A/2615, 7 December 1953), 16–18.

141 *Ibid.*, 27.

142 United Nations, *Statute of the Administrative Tribunal*, Art. 10, par. 2.

143 *Ibid.*, Art. 12.

144 *Reed*, 51 JUNAT 248-250 (1953).

145 *Bulsara* (AT/DEC/73, 5 December 1958), 2.

146 United Nations, General Assembly, *Report of the Special Committee on Review of Administrative Tribunal Judgments* (A/2909, 10 June 1955), 1–52. See also *idem, Report of the Special Committee on Review of Administrative Tribunal Judgments: Report of the Fifth Committee* (A/3016, 5 November 1955), 1.

147 *Ibid.*, (A/3016), 1–2.

148 *Ibid.*, 2.

149 *Ibid.*, 3.

150 *Ibid.*, 3–4.

151 *Ibid.*, 4.

152 *Ibid.*, 4–5.

153 *Ibid.*, 6–7.

154 *Ibid.*, 7.

155 *Ibid.*, 7–8.

156 *Ibid.*, 8–9.

157 *Ibid.*, 9–10.

158 *Ibid.*, 11–21. See also United Nations, General Assembly, *Official Records: Tenth Session*, Supplement No. 19 (Resolutions adopted by the General Assembly during its Tenth Session, from 20 September to 20 December 1955) (A/3116, 1955), 30.

159 United Nations, *Statute of the Administrative Tribunal*, Art. 11, pars. 1 and 4.

160 *Ibid.*, Art. 11, pars. 2 and 3.

161 *Ibid.*, Art. 11, pars. 3 and 5.

162 United Nations, General Assembly, Committee on Applications for Review of Administrative Tribunal Judgments, *Administrative Tribunal Judgment No. 64: Stepczynski against the Secretary-General of the United Nations* (Report of the Committee) (A/AC.86/1, 26 October 1956), 1–2.

163 See A/AC.86/3–7, 5 February 1957–10 February 1959.

CHAPTER 5

1 Sydney D. Bailey, *The General Assembly of the United Nations: A Study of Procedure and Practice* (New York: Praeger, 1960), 256.

2 *Ibid.*, 257.

3 Glendon Schubert, "Behavioral Research in Public Law," *American Political Science Review*, LVII (1963), 433–45.

4 C. Herman Pritchett, *The Roosevelt Court: A Study in Judicial Politics and Values, 1937–1947* (New York: Macmillan, 1948).

5 C. Herman Pritchett, *Civil Liberties and the Vinson Court* (Chicago: University of Chicago Press, 1954).

6 Glendon Schubert, *Quantitative Analysis of Judicial Behavior* (Glencoe, Illinois: The Free Press, 1959).

7 Robert V. Presthus and Sevda Erem, *Statistical Analysis in Comparative Administration: The Turkish Conseil d'Etat* (Ithaca: Cornell University Press, 1958).

8 Sir Gerald G. Fitzmaurice, *The British Year Book of International Law*, "The Law and Procedure of the International Court of Justice: General Principles and Substantive Law," XXVII (1950), 1–41; "The Law and Procedure of the International Court of Justice: Treaty Interpretation and Certain Other Treaty Points," XXVIII (1951), 1–28; "The Law and Procedure of the International Court of Justice: International Organizations and Tribunals," XXIX (1952), 1–62; "The Law and Procedure of the International Court of Justice, 1951–1954: General Principles and Sources of Law," XXX (1953), 1–70; "The Law and Procedure of the International Court of Justice, 1951–54; Points of Substantive Law, Part I," XXXI (1954), 371–429; "The Law and Procedure of the International Court of Justice, 1951–54: Points of Substantive Law, Part II," XXXII (1955–56), 20–96; "The Law and Procedure of the International Court of Justice, 1951–54: Treaty Interpretation and Other Treaty Points," XXXIII (1957), 203–93; "The Law and Procedure of the International Court of Justice, 1951–54: Questions of Jurisdiction, Competence and Procedure," XXXIV (1958), 1–161; and "The Law and Procedure of the International Court of Justice, 1954–59: General Principles and Sources of International Law," XXXV (1959), 183–231.

9 Fitzmaurice, *British Year Book of International Law*, XXVII (1950), 1.

10 Admittedly, these categories are to some extent arbitrary, because their respective boundaries are far from clear-cut. Thus, to a large degree, the second and third categories are two sides of the same coin. Notwithstanding this, it is both possible and analytically convenient to make such a three-fold classification.

11 For an excellent analysis of his political power, see Stephen M. Schwebel, *The Secretary-General of the United Nations: His Political Powers and Practice* (Cambridge: Harvard University Press, 1952).

12 *Ibid.*, 44.

13 *Howrani et al.*, 4 JUNAT 10 (1951).

14 *Aubert et al.*, 2 JUNAT 4 (1950).

15 *De Pojidaeff*, 17 JUNAT 63 (1952).

16 *Levinson*, 43 JUNAT 213 (1953); *Bergh*, 44 JUNAT 219 (1953); *Mohan*, 45 JUNAT 223 (1953); *White*, 46 JUNAT 228 (1953); *Carter*, 47 JUNAT 232 (1953), *Carruthers*, 49 JUNAT 242 (1953); and *Davidian* (AT/DEC/75, 5 December 1958), 7.

17 *Vanhove*, 14 JUNAT 41 (1952).

18 *Aubert et al.*, 2 JUNAT 4 (1950). See also *Carson* (AT/DEC/85, 14 September 1962), 7.

19 *Howrani et al.*, 4 JUNAT 11 (1951).

20 *Ibid.*, 12.

21 *Kaplan*, 19 JUNAT 75 (1953). Italics mine. See also *Crawford*, 18 JUNAT 68 (1953); *Rubin*, 21 JUNAT 84 (1953); *Kagen-Pozner*, 22 JUNAT 89 (1953); *Sokolow*, 23 JUNAT 94 (1953); *Saperstein*, 24 JUNAT 99 (1953); *Van Tassel*, 25 JUNAT 104 (1953); *Zap, M.*, 26 JUNAT 109 (1953); *Zap, H.*, 27 JUNAT 113 (1953); *Levinson*, 43 JUNAT 213 (1953); *Bergh*, 44 JUNAT 217; *Mohan* 45 JUNAT 222 (1953); *Wang*, 48 JUNAT 236 (1953); *Carruthers*, 49 JUNAT 241 (1953); *Brown*, 50 JUNAT 246 (1953); *Mauch*, 54 JUNAT 273 (1954); *Chattopadhyay*, 58 JUNAT 312 (1955); and *Chiacchia* (AT/DEC/90, 29 November 1963), 7.

22 *Mauch*, 54 JUNAT 272 (1954).

23 *Aglion,* 56 JUNAT 290 (1954).
24 *Ball,* 60 JUNAT 330 (1955).
25 *Gordon,* 29 JUNAT 123 (1953).
26 *Ibid.* See also *Svenchansky,* 30 JUNAT 131 (1953); *Harris,* 31 JUNAT 139 (1953); *Eldridge,* 32 JUNAT 147 (1953); *Glassman,* 33 JUNAT 155 (1953); *Older,* 34 JUNAT 163 (1953); *Bancroft,* 35 JUNAT 171–172 (1953); *Elveson,* 36 JUNAT 179 (1953); *Reed,* 37 JUNAT 187 (1953); and *Carson* (AT/DEC/85, 14 September 1962), 9.
27 *Miss Y* (AT/DEC/83, 8 December 1961), 9–11.
28 *Carson* (AT/DEC/85, 14 September 1962), 8.
29 *Glaser,* 38 JUNAT 196–198 (1953).
30 *Wallach,* 53 JUNAT 264 (1954).
31 Friedmann and Fatouros, "United Nations Administrative Tribunal," 25.
32 *Rubin,* 21 JUNAT 84–85 (1953).
33 Friedmann and Fatouros, "United Nations Administrative Tribunal," 26 and *Rubin,* 21 JUNAT 85 (1953).
34 Friedmann and Fatouros, "United Nations Administrative Tribunal," 26.
35 *Rubin,* 21 JUNAT 80 (1953); *Saperstein,* 24 JUNAT 95 (1953); *Gordon,* 29 JUNAT 120 (1953); *Svenchansky,* 30 JUNAT 128 (1953); *Harris,* 31 JUNAT 135 (1953); *Eldridge,* 32 JUNAT 144 (1953); *Glassman,* 33 JUNAT 151 (1953); *Older,* 34 JUNAT 160 (1953); *Bancroft,* 35 JUNAT 168 (1953); *Elveson,* 36 JUNAT 176 (1953); *Reed,* 37 JUNAT 184 (1953); and *Glaser,* 38 JUNAT 192 (1953).
36 *Aubert et al.,* 2 JUNAT 5 (1950).
37 *Gordon,* 29 JUNAT 122–127 (1953). See also Judgments Nos. 30–37. Cited in note 35, *supra.*
38 *De Ungria* (AT/DEC/71, 3 December 1958), 7.
39 *Kaplan,* 19 JUNAT 73–74 (1953). See also *Middleton,* 20 JUNAT 76 (1953); *Rubin,* 21 JUNAT 80 (1953); *Kagen-Pozner,* 22 JUNAT 86 (1953); *Sokolow,* 23 JUNAT 91 (1953); *Saperstein,* 24 JUNAT 95 (1953); *Zap, H.,* 27 JUNAT 110 (1953); and *Wallach,* 53 JUNAT 260 (1954).
40 *Kaplan,* 19 JUNAT 74 (1953).
41 Friedmann and Fatouros, "United Nations Administrative Tribunal," 24–25.
42 *Crawford,* 18 JUNAT 65 (1953); *Gordon,* 29 JUNAT 120 (1953); *Svenchansky,* 30 JUNAT 128 (1953); *Harris,* 31 JUNAT 135 (1953); *Eldridge,* 32 JUNAT 144 (1953); *Glassman,* 33 JUNAT 151 (1953); *Older,* 34 JUNAT 160 (1953); *Bancroft,* 35 JUNAT 168 (1953); *Elveson,* 36 JUNAT 176 (1953); *Reed,* 37 JUNAT 184 (1953); *Glaser,* 38 JUNAT 192 (1953); *Eldridge,* 39 JUNAT 199 (1953); *Svenchansky,* 40 JUNAT 202 (1953); *Glaser,* 41 JUNAT 205 (1953); *Crawford,* 42 JUNAT 207 (1953); *Crawford et al.,* 61 JUNAT 331; and *Carson* (AT/DEC/85, 14 September 1962).
43 *Champoury* (AT/DEC/76, 17 August 1959); *Coffinet* (AT/DEC/77, 17 August 1959); *Ducret* (AT/DEC/78, 17 August 1959); *Fath* (AT/DEC/79, 17 August 1959); and *Snape* (AT/DEC/80, 17 August 1959).
44 *Puvrez* (AT/DEC/82, 4 December 1961), 13.
45 *Reed,* 37 JUNAT 191–192 (1953).
46 *Young* (AT/DEC/84, 11 September 1962).
47 *Julhiard,* 62 JUNAT 345 (1955).
48 Quoted in *Radspieler* (AT/DEC/72, 3 December 1958), 6.
49 *Ibid.,* 6–9.
50 *Crawford,* 18 JUNAT 65 (1953); *Kaplan,* 19 JUNAT 71 (1953); *Middleton,* 20 JUNAT 76 (1953); *Rubin,* 21 JUNAT 80 (1953); *Kagen-Pozner,* 22 JUNAT 86 (1953); *Sokolow,* 23 JUNAT 91 (1953); *Saperstein,* 24 JUNAT 95 (1953); *Van Tassel,* 25 JUNAT 101 (1953); *Zap, M.,* 26 JUNAT

106 (1953); *Zap, H.,* 27 JUNAT 110 (1953); *Wallach,* 28 JUNAT 114 (1953); *Gordon,* 29 JUNAT 120 (1953); *Svenchansky,* 30 JUNAT 128 (1953); *Harris,* 31 JUNAT 135 (1953); *Eldridge,* 32 JUNAT 144 (1953); *Glassman,* 33 JUNAT 151 (1953); *Older,* 34 JUNAT 160 (1953); *Bancroft,* 35 JUNAT 168 (1953); *Elveson,* 36 JUNAT 176 (1953); *Reed,* 37 JUNAT 184 (1953); *Glaser,* 38 JUNAT 192 (1953); *Eldridge,* 39 JUNAT 199 (1953); *Svenchansky,* 40 JUNAT 202 (1953); *Glaser,* 41 JUNAT 205 (1953); *Crawford,* 42 JUNAT 207 (1953); *Reed,* 51 JUNAT 247 (1953); *Wallach,* 53 JUNAT 260 (1954); *Crawford et al.,* 61 JUNAT 331 (1955); and *Harris et al.,* 67 JUNAT 388 (1956). Of these, Judgments Nos. 18 and 28 to 42 are in favor of the applicants.

51 Bancroft, Frank C.; Crawford, Ruth E.; Eldridge, Hope T.; Elveson, Leon; Glaser, Eda; Glassman, Sidney; Gordon, Joel; Harris, Jack S.; Kagen-Pozner, Helen; Kaplan, Irwing; Middleton, Mary A.; Older, Julia; Reed, Jane; Rubin, Martin H.; Saperstein, Celia; Sokolow, Sonya J.; Svenchansky, Alexander; Van Tassel, Alfred J.; Wallach, Eugene; Zap, Herman; and Zap, Marjorie L.

52 The amendment reads in part, ". . . nor shall [any person] be compelled in any Criminal Case to be a witness against himself . . ."

53 *Gordon,* 29 JUNAT 120–121 (1953).

54 *Ibid.,* 121.

55 *Ibid.*

56 *Ibid.,* 122.

57 *Ibid.,* 122–23.

58 *Ibid.,* 123.

59 Staff Regulation 1.4 reads in part: "Members of the Secretariat shall conduct themselves at all times in a manner befitting their status as international civil servants. They shall not engage in any activity that is incompatible with the proper discharge of their duties with the United Nations. They shall avoid any action and in particular any kind of public pronouncement which may adversely reflect on their status, or on the integrity, independence and impartiality which are required by their status . . . ."

60 *Gordon,* 29 JUNAT 124–125 (1953).

61 *Ibid.,* 125.

62 *Ibid.,* 125–26.

63 *Ibid.,* 126.

64 *Ibid.,* 126–27.

65 *Kaplan,* 19 JUNAT 71 (1953); *Middleton,* 20 JUNAT 76 (1953); *Rubin,* 21 JUNAT 80 (1953); *Kagen-Pozner,* 22 JUNAT 86 (1953); *Sokolow,* 23 JUNAT 91 (1953); *Saperstein,* 24 JUNAT 95 (1953); *Van Tassel,* 25 JUNAT 101 (1953); *Zap, M.,* 26 JUNAT 106 (1953); and *Zap, H.,* 27 JUNAT 110 (1953).

66 *I.C.J. Reports 1954,* 48.

67 *Ibid.,* 51–53.

68 *Ibid.,* 53. Italics mine.

69 *Ibid.*

70 *Ibid.,* 55–56.

71 *Ibid.,* 57.

72 *Ibid.,* 57–58.

73 *Ibid.,* 59.

74 *Ibid.,* 61.

75 *Ibid.,* 62.

76 *Ibid.,* 90.

77 *Ibid.,* 90–91.

BIBLIOGRAPHY

PUBLIC DOCUMENTS

Food and Agriculture Organization, Conference. *Administrative Tribunal and Appeals Procedure*: Extract from Report of Council of FAO: Seventh Session, 14–17 November 1949 (FA) C49/III/3, 21 November 1949).

International Court of Justice. *Statute of the International Court of Justice.*

——. "Reparation for injuries suffered in the service of the United Nations, Advisory Opinion," *I.C.J. Reports 1949*, 1–174.

——. "Effect of awards of compensation made by the U.N. Administrative Tribunal, Advisory Opinion of July 13th, 1954," *I.C.J. Reports 1954*, 47–97.

——. "Judgments of the Administrative Tribunal of the I.L.O. upon complaints made against the UNESCO, Advisory Opinion of October 23rd, 1956," *I.C.J. Reports 1956*, 77–95.

United Nations. *Charter.*

——. *Repertory of Practice of United Nations Organs.* Vol. V. New York, 1955.

United Nations, Administrative Tribunal. *Competence of the Administrative Tribunal to Award Costs: Memorandum submitted by the Legal Department.* A/CN.5/5, 13 December 1950.

——. *Judgments of the United Nations Administrative Tribunal, Numbers 1 to 70, 1950–1957.* AT/DEC/1 to 70, 1958.

——. *Judgments Nos. 71 to 90.* AT/DEC/71–90, 3 December 1958–29 November 1963.

——.*Verbatim Records.* A/CN.5/PV 1–4 and AT/PV/5–86, 1950–1962.

——. *Statute and Rules*: Provisions in force with effect from 1 November 1962. AT/11/Rev. 2, 1962.

United Nations, General Assembly. *Acceptance by the Specialized Agencies of the Jurisdiction of the United Nations Administrative Tribunal in Matters Involving Applications Alleging Non-Observance of the Regulations of the United Nations Joint Staff Pension Fund: Report of the Secretary-General.* A/2970, 19 September 1955.

————. *Administrative Tribunal: Report of the Secretary-General.* A/91, 16 October 1946.

————. *Adoption of the Agenda of the Seventeenth Regular Session, Allocation of Items, and Organization of the Session: First Report of the General Committee.* A/5230, 21 September 1962.

————. *Appointments to Fill Vacancies in the Membership of Subsidiary Bodies of the General Assembly: Administrative Tribunal* (Note by the Secretariat). A/C.5/L.752 and 753, 21 November 1962.

————. *Appointments to Fill Vacancies in the Membership of Subsidiary Bodies of the General Assembly: United Nations Administrative Tribunal* (Report of the Fifth Committee). A/5295, 29 November 1962.

————. *Budget Estimates for the Financial Year 1961: Payment of honorarium to members of the Administrative Tribunal* (Report of the Secretary-General). A/C.5/814, 4 May 1960.

————. *Budget Estimates for the Financial Year 1961: Payment of honoraria to the members of the Administrative Tribunal* (Report of the Fifth Committee). A/4609, 2 December 1960.

————. *Budget Estimates for the Financial Year 1963: Report of the Fifth Committee.* A/539, 19 December 1962.

————. *Establishment of an Administrative Tribunal: Report of the Secretary-General.* A/986, 21 September 1949.

————. *Establishment of an Administrative Tribunal: Draft Report of the Fifth Committee.* A/C.5/L.41, 21 November 1949.

————. *Establishment of an Administrative Tribunal: Fifth report of 1949 of the Advisory Committee on Administrative and Budgetary Questions.* A/1003, 28 September 1949.

————. *Establishment of an Administrative Tribunal: Note by the Secretary-General.* A/C.5/304, 29 September 1949.

————. *Establishment of an Administrative Tribunal: Note Submitted by the WHO.* A/C.5/L.21, 2 November 1949.

————. *Establishment of an Administrative Tribunal: Report of the Fifth Committee.* A/1127, 22 November 1949.

————. *Establishment of an Administrative Tribunal: Belgium, Egypt, France, Netherlands, Venezuela: Amendments to the draft statute of the Administrative Tribunal proposed by the Fifth Committee.* A/1132, 23 November 1949.

————. *Establishment of a United Nations Administrative Tribunal: Resolution adopted by the General Assembly at its 255th plenary meeting on 24 November 1949.* A/1142, 25 November 1949.

————. *Establishment of an Administrative Tribunal: Appointment of Members.* A/C.5/L.45, 5 December 1949.

————. *Note by the Secretary-General.* A/INF/52, 30 December 1952.

————. *Organization and Administration of the Secretariat: Report of the Fifth Committee.* A/273, 13 December 1946.

————. *Official Records: Sixth Session,* Supplement No. 1 (Annual Report of the Secretary-General on the Work of the Organization, 1 July 1949-30 June 1950.) A/1287, 1950.

————. *Official Records: Tenth Session,* Supplement No. 19 (Resolutions adopted by the General Assembly during its Tenth Session from 20 September-20 December 1955). A/ 3116, 1955.

————. *Official Records: Fifteenth Session,* Supplement No. 7 (Advisory Committee on Administrative and Budgetary Questions, First Report to the General Assembly at its Fifteenth Session). A/4408, 1960.

————. *Provisional Summary Record: Fifth Committee.* AC.5/SR 187, 188, 189, 190, 214, 215, 216, and 221; 29 September to 8 November 1949.

————. *Verbatim Record of the Two Hundred and Fifty-Fifth Plenary Meeting: Fourth Session.* A/PV 255, 24 November 1949.

————. *Verbatim Record of the Two Hundred and Seventy-Fourth Plenary Meeting, Fourth Session.* A/PV 274, 9 December 1949.

————. *Provisional Verbatim Records of the Eleven Hundred and Ninety-First Plenary Meeting, Seventeenth Session.* A/PV 1191, 11 December 1962.

————. *Report of the Secretary-General on Personnel Policy.* A/2533, 2 November 1953.

————. *Personnel Policy of the United Nations: Note by the Secretary-General.* A/C.5/561, 16 November 1953.

————. *Personnel Policy: Reports of the Secretary-General and the Advisory Committee on Administrative and Budgetary Questions* (Report of the Fifth Committee). A/2615, 7 December 1953.

————. *Report of the Special Committee on Review of Administrative Tribunal Judgments.* A/2909, 10 June 1955.

————. *Report of the Special Committee on Review of Administrative Tribunal Judgments: Report of the Fifth Committee.* A/3016, 5 November 1955.

————. *Report of the Committee on Special Administrative Questions: Report of the Fifth Committee.* A/2539, 2 November 1953.

————. *UN Salary, Allowances and Benefits Systems: Report of the Salary Review Committee.* A/3209, 18 October 1956.

United Nations, General Assembly, Committee on Applications for Review of Administrative Tribunal Judgments. *Administrative Tribunal Judgment No. 64: Stepczynski against the Secretary-General of the United Nations* (Report of the Committee). A/AC.86/1, 26 October 1956.

United Nations, Preparatory Commission. *Report of the Executive Committee.* PC/EX/113/Rev.1, 12 November 1945.

————. *Administrative Tribunal: Report of Committee 6.* PC/AB/45, 15 December 1945.

————. *Report of Committee 6.* PC/AB/56/Rev.2, 22 December 1945.

United Nations, Secretariat. *Administrative Manual.* UNST (O2) A2, n.d.
————. *Staff Rules: Staff Regulations of the United Nations and Staff Rules* 101.1 to 112.8 (Secretary-General's Bulletin). ST/SGB/Staff Rules/1, 16 March 1962.
————. *Representation by Counsel in Disciplinary and Appeal Cases: An Administrative Instruction issued by the Secretary-General to members of the Staff.* ST/AI/153, 7 March 1963.
————. *Membership of the Panel of Counsel in Disciplinary and Appeal Cases: An Information Circular issued by the Director of Personnel to members of the staff.* ST/ADM/SER.A/833, 7 March 1963.
United States Civil Service Commission. *Civil Service News* (news release), March 28, 1962. Washington, 1962.

BOOKS

Bailey, Sydney D. *The General Assembly of the United Nations: A Study of Procedure and Practice.* New York: Praeger, 1960.
————. *The Secretariat of the United Nations.* New York: Carnegie Endowment for International Peace, 1962.
Bedjaoui, Mohammed. *Fonction Publique Internationale et Influences Nationales.* London: Stevens & Sons Ltd., 1958.
Blau, Peter M. *The Dynamics of Bureaucracy: A Study of Interpersonal Relations in Two Governmental Agencies.* Chicago: University of Chicago Press, 1953.
Briggs, Herbert W. (ed.) *The Law of Nations: Cases, Documents, and Notes.* 2nd ed.; New York: Appleton-Century-Crofts, Inc., 1952.
Campbell, G. A. *The Civil Service in Britain.* Harmondsworth, Middlesex: Penguin Books Ltd., 1955.
Chapman, Brian. *The Profession of Government.* London: George Allen & Unwin Ltd., 1959.
Claude, Inis L., Jr. *Swords into Plowshare: The Problems and Progress of International Organization.* 2nd. ed.; New York: Random House, 1959.
Corbett, Percy E. *Law and Society in the Relations of States.* New York: Harcourt, Brace & Co., 1951.
Finer, Herman. *Theory and Practice of Modern Government.* Rev. ed.; New York: Henry, Holt & Co., 1950.
————. *Governments of Greater European Powers.* New York: Henry, Holt & Co., 1956.
Gellhorn, Walter, and Clark Byse. *Administrative Law: Cases and Comments.* Brooklyn: The Foundation Press, 1960.
Gerth, Hans, and C. Wright Mills. (trans. & eds.) *From Max Weber: Essays in Sociology.* New York: Oxford University Press, 1946.
Gladden, E. N. *Civil Service or Bureaucracy.* London: Staples Press, Ltd., 1956.
Hammarskjöld, Dag. *The International Civil Servant in Law and in Fact.* London: Oxford University Press, 1961.

Hamsen, C. J. *Executive Discretion and Judicial Control.* London: Stevens & Sons Ltd., 1954.

Hart, James. *An Introduction to Administrative Law: With Selected Cases.* New York: F. S. Crofts & Co., 1940.

Herzberg, Frederick, et al. *Job Attitudes: Review of Research and Opinion.* Pittsburgh: Psychological Service of Pittsburgh, 1957.

Herzberg, Frederick, Bernard Mausner, and Barbara Block Snyderman. *The Motivation to Work.* 2nd ed.; New York: John Wiley & Sons, Inc., 1959.

Hudson, Manley O. *International Tribunals: Past and Future.* New York: Carnegie Endowment for International Peace, 1944.

Jeanneau, Benoit. *Les Principes Generaux du Droit dans la Jurisprudence Administrative.* Paris, 1954.

Jenks, C. Wilfred. *The Proper Law of International Organisations.* London: Stevens & Sons, Ltd., 1962.

Jessup, Philip C. *Transnational Law.* New Haven: Yale University Press, 1956.

Kaplan, H. Eliot. *The Law of Civil Service.* New York: Mathew Bender & Co., 1958.

Loveday, A. *Reflections on International Administration.* London: Oxford University Press, 1956.

Marvick, Dwaine. *Career Perspectives in a Bureaucratic Setting.* Ann Arbor: University of Michigan Press, 1954.

Presthus, Robert V., and Sevda Erem. *Statistical Analysis in Comparative Administration: The Turkish Conseil d'Etat.* Ithaca: Cornell University Press, 1958.

Pritchett, C. Herman. *The Roosevelt Court: A Study in Judicial Politics and Values, 1937–1947.* New York: Macmillan Co., 1948.

————. *Civil Liberties and the Vinson Court.* Chicago: University of Chicago Press, 1954.

Rosenne, Shabtai. *The International Court of Justice: An Essay in Political and Legal Theory.* Leyden, the Netherlands: A. W. Sijthoff's Uitgeversmaatschappij N. V., 1957.

Schubert, Glendon. *Quantitative Analysis of Judicial Behavior.* Glencoe, Ill.: The Free Press, 1959.

Schwebel, Stephen M. *The Secretary-General of the United Nations: His Political Powers and Practice.* Cambridge: Harvard University Press, 1952.

Stahl, O. Glenn. *Public Personnel Administration.* 4th ed.; New York: Harper, 1956.

Van Riper, Paul P. *History of the United States Civil Service.* Evanston: Row, Peterson & Co., 1958.

Viteles, Morris S. *Motivation and Morale in Industry.* New York: W. W. Norton & Co., 1953.

Walker, Nigel. *Morale in the Civil Service: A Study of the Desk Worker.* Edinburgh: Edinburgh University Press, 1961.

170 *Bibliography*

Weber, Max. *The Theory of Social and Economic Organization.* trans. A. M. Henderson, and Talcott Parsons. New York: Oxford University Press, 1947.

Wright, Quincy, *Contemporary International Law: A Balance Sheet.* Rev. ed.; New York: Random House, 1961.

Young, Tien–Cheng. *International Civil Service: Principles and Problems.* Brussels: International Institute of Administrative Sciences, 1958.

Zink, Harold. *Modern Governments.* Princeton: D. Van Nostrand Co., Inc., 1958.

ARTICLES

Bastid, Suzanne. "Statut Juridique de Fonctionnaires des Nations Unies," in G. H. J. Van Der Molen, W. P. J. Pompe, and J. H. W. Verziji (eds.) *The United Nations: Ten Years' Legal Progress.* Hague: Nederlandse Studentenvereniging voor Wereldrechtsorde, 1956, 145–65.

———. "Les Tribunaux Administratifs Internationaux et Leur Jurisprudence," *Recueil des cours.* XCII, Pt. 2 (1957), 347–517.

Briggs, Herbert W. "New Dimensions in International Law," *American Political Science Review.* XLVI (1952), 677–98.

Chatenet, P. "The Civil Service in France," in William A. Robson (ed.) *The Civil Service in Britain and France.* London: The Hogarth Press, 1956, 164–88.

Claude, Inis L., Jr. "The United Nations and the Use of Force," *International Conciliation,* No. 532 (1961), 325–84.

Diamant, Alfred. "The French Administrative System: The Republic Passes but the Administration Remains," in William J. Siffin (ed.) *Toward the Comparative Study of Public Administration.* Bloomington: Department of Government, Indiana University, 1957, 182–218.

Fitzmaurice, Gerald G., Sir. "The Law and Procedure of the International Court of Justice: General Principles and Substantive Law," *British Year Book of International Law,* XXVII (1950), 1–41.

Friedmann, Wolfgang, and Fatouros, Arghyrios A. "The United Nations Administrative Tribunal," *International Organization,* XI (1957), 13–29.

Lengyel, Peter. "Some Trends in the International Civil Service," *International Organization,* XIII (1959), 520–37.

Loveday, A. "Staff Salaries in the UN Family," *International Organization,* XI (1957), 635–48.

Schubert, Glendon. "Behavioral Research in Public Law," *American Political Science Review,* LVII (1963), 433–45.

Swift, Richard N. "Personnel Problems and the United Nations Secretariat," *International Organization,* XI (1957), 228–47.

UNPUBLISHED MATERIAL

Choi, Woonsang. "The Legal Regulation of Employment Relations within International Organizations." J. S. D. dissertation, Harvard Law School, 1960.

OTHER SOURCES

Morgenthau, Hans J. "Dilemmas of American Foreign Policy," lecture delivered at Cornell University, March, 1963.

United Nations Administrative Tribunal, New York. Personal interviews with Dr. Nicholas Teslenko, Executive Secretary of the Tribunal. December, 1962 and April and July, 1963.

INDEX

Administrative Instruction, 81
Administrative Manual 80, 158, *n*99
Advisory Committee on Administrative and Budgetary Questions, 8, 41–42, 55
Advisory Committee on a Statute of a United Nations Administrative Tribunal: creation of, 34–35; work of, 35–38; draft statute prepared by, 35–38; mentioned, 53
Applications instituting proceedings: required form and content of, 69–71; pleas, 70; explanatory statement, 70
Applications: reasons given for rejection of, 104–105
Appointment and Promotion Board, 12

Bailey, Sydney D., 10, 11, 96
Bastid, Mme. Paul, 4, 25, 26, 33, 51, 57, 78, 82, 83
Bedjaoui, Mohammed, 5
Blau, Peter M., 21
Briggs, Herbert W., 6
British Year Book of International Law, 105

Choi, Woonsang, 5
Claude, Inis L., Jr., 3, 6
Committee of Experts on Salary, Allowances and Leave Systems, 114
Committee on Applications for Review of Administrative Tribunal Judgments, 94, 95
Common-law, 83

Competence: definition of, 63; distinction between competence and jurisdiction, 62–63; categories of, 63–64; competence *ratione materiae*, 64, 66; competence *ratione personae*, 64–66; competence *ratione temporis*, 38, 64, 67; competence to award costs, 67; competence to decide disputes regarding competence, 67; competence to interpret judgments, 67; quasi-appellate competence of the International Court of Justice over judgments of the U.N. Administrative Tribunal, 89
Conseil d'Etat, French, 22, 25, 82
Conseil d'Etat, Turkish, 97–98
Contractual elements, 112

Disciplinary measures, 16
Disputes, types of, 98–99
Drug Supervisory Body, 55, 56

Egyptian labor law, 81
Employment contract: types of, 11; nature of, 80
Employment disputes: need for adjustment of, 33
Employment relations, law of, 127
Employment security: meaning and implications of, 19–22; criteria of, 20; effects on worker's attitude, 20; as guaranteed in France, Great Britain, and the United States, 22; desirability of, 22; extent of, in the

LOUISIANA STATE UNIVERSITY STUDIES

The Studies was established to publish the results of research by faculty members, staff, and graduate students of the University. Manuscripts of exceptional merit from sources other than aforementioned are considered for publication provided they deal with subjects of particular interest to Louisiana.

The Studies originally appeared as a unified series consisting of forty-two numbers, published between the years 1931 and 1941. In 1951 the Studies was reactivated, and is now being issued in the following series: Social Sciences, Humanities, Biological Sciences, Physical Sciences, and Coastal Studies. Other series may be established as the need arises.